PROBLEM-SOLVING TRAINING

Mark Amendola & Robert Oliver, Series Editors

Kim Parker • Robert Calame • Knut Kornelius Gundersen
Andrew Simon • John Choi • Mark Amendola

RESEARCH PRESS
PUBLISHERS

2612 North Mattis Avenue, Champaign, Illinois 61822
800.519.2707 / researchpress.com

RESEARCH PRESS
PUBLISHERS

Prepare and *Skillstreaming* are the registered copyright of Research Press. *Aggression Replacement Training* and *ART* are the registered copyrights of Dr. Barry Glick.

PDF versions of forms and handouts included in this book are available for download on the book webpage at **www.researchpress.com/downloads**

Copies of this book may be ordered from Research Press at the address given on the title page.

Composition by Jeff Helgesen
Cover design by McKenzie Wagner, Inc.
Printed by Seaway Printing, Inc.

ISBN 978-0-87822-679-5
Library of Congress Control Number 2013946193

Contents

Tables

Foreword

The optimal intervention package is never final or complete . . . intervention approaches must perpetually evolve. —Arnold P. Goldstein

The legacy of Arnold P. Goldstein (1933–2002) spans a remarkable career, blending science with practice to address the most pressing problems of modern youth. The bookends of Arnie's shelf of writings both concern the theme of lasting behavior change. A half century ago, he joined Kenneth Heller and Lee Sechrest as they mined experimental and cognitive research for secrets of how learning endures. In two final books, he set the challenge for the decades ahead: What methods yield lasting change? And how do we engage resistant youth as partners in the process of change?

There are 300 approaches to control student violence, Arnie mused, most based on hearsay, hope, and desperation. While such behavior is challenging to change, most real-world programs are punitive, permissive, or defeatist. For example, he questioned attempts in recent years to portray gangs as narrowly pathological, thereby justifying coercive policies. All adolescents seek out peers for satisfaction, and gang membership is seldom exclusively destructive, but offers camaraderie, pride, excitement, and identity.

The strengths perspective was central to Arnie's philosophy. Seeing potential in all youth motivated his efforts to turn negative peer groups into "prosocial gangs." He was intrigued by the idea that youth themselves may be credible experts on delinquency. This respect for the voices of youth was exemplified in his book *Delinquents on Delinquency* (Goldstein, 1990). Always open to multiple perspectives, he saw ordinary knowledge as a useful adjunct to professional scientific knowledge.

While some feared that aggregating troubled youth for treatment would lead to peer deviance training, Arnie welcomed the opportunity to work with delinquents as a group. It was his understanding of the power of the friendship group that enabled Aggression Replacement Training (ART) to penetrate the gang culture (Goldstein & Glick, 1987). He recognized the potential of building positive youth cultures through peer helping. In fact, he cited research showing that youth were more motivated to participate in skill instruction if they thought they could use this information to help their peers, a concept that served as the foundation of the EQUIP Program (Gibbs, Potter, & Goldstein, 1995).

From Arnie's earliest writings, respectful relationships were recognized as the foundation of all successful helping encounters. This universal principle made his interventions relevant across diverse domains of education, prevention, treatment, and corrections. His research showed that it was just as important to enhance the attractiveness of the helper as to try to change the helpee. While many traditional approaches for troubled youth saw them as "perpetrators," Arnie embraced Kurt Lewin's interactionist approach: Behavior is a function of a person interacting with an environment, which Arnie called the "person-environment duet." If the person is to change, the ecology must be changed.

Finally, Arnie had little time for holy wars among behavioral, cognitive, and developmental perspectives. Instead, he sought to integrate wisdom from these diverse theories. With all of his behavioral expertise, he was among the first to recognize the modest potency of social skills training in isolation. Thus, in ART he added anger management and moral reasoning and designed interventions attuned to the ecology of children and youth. Employing many methods for many needs, he created powerful evidence-based interventions long before the notion was in style. ART evolved into the initial edition of *The Prepare Curriculum* in 1988, revised in 1999. Arnie realized that if we are to meet the needs of those we serve, strategies need to be prescriptive in nature. Thus Prepare provided additional resources to assist change agents. This Prepare Curriculum Implementation Guide provides practitioners with a practical outline for implementing these strategies, in a user friendly, evidence-based manner. In this spirit, those of us who follow in the footsteps of Arnold Goldstein continue the search for methods that create deep learning and enduring change.

LARRY K. BRENDTRO, PHD
STARR COMMONWEALTH INSTITUTE FOR TRAINING
ALBION, MICHIGAN

References

Gibbs, J. C., Potter, G. B., & Goldstein, A. P. (1995). *The EQUIP Program: Teaching youth to think and act responsibly through a peer-helping approach.* Champaign, IL: Research Press.

Goldstein, A. P. (1988). *The Prepare Curriculum: Teaching prosocial competencies.* Champaign, IL: Research Press.

Goldstein, A. P. (1990). *Delinquents on delinquency.* Champaign, IL: Research Press.

Goldstein, A. P. (1999). *The Prepare Curriculum: Teaching prosocial competencies* (Rev. ed.). Champaign, IL: Research Press.

Goldstein, A. P., & Glick, B. (1987). *Aggression Replacement Training: A comprehensive intervention for aggressive youth.* Champaign, IL: Research Press.

Preface

In September of 2001, at a meeting of practitioners from all over the world held in Malmo, Sweden, Arnold P. Goldstein made clear his charge: The strategies and techniques he described in *The Prepare Curriculum: Teaching Prosocial Competencies* (Goldstein, 1988, 1999) were just the beginning. He challenged all in attendance to continue to develop his ideas through their own work and to share best practices to continue to grow the Prepare Curriculum.

As described in the introduction to this book, contributed by Clive R. Hollin, the Prepare Curriculum includes coordinated psychoeducational courses designed to teach prosocial competencies to adolescents and younger children who struggle with various aspects of social and emotional behavior. The curriculum is still widely in use; however, Prepare methods have evolved over the years, resulting in many useful adaptations and expansions. Organizations and research groups formed to share ideas. The United States Center for Aggression Replacement Training ultimately developed into a worldwide network of researchers and practitioners known as ICART (International Center for Aggression Replacement Training), appointed by Arnold Goldstein with the aim of promoting quality control, further development, and continued dissemination of his programs. ICART evolved into PREPSEC (PRepare for Evidence-based Practice in Social Emotional Competency) International, a special interest organization designed to promote and expand Arnold P. Goldstein's combinations of programs for training in social competencies based on the Prepare Curriculum and other programs of a similar nature.

Likewise, this and other Prepare Curriculum Implementation Guides are intended to further Arnold Goldstein's original work—specifically, by describing and giving direction to the continued expansion of the Prepare methods. In conjunction with the original curriculum, the guides are designed to offer practitioners coherent, evidence-based approaches to enhancing the prosocial abilities of young people. We will be forever grateful to Dr. Goldstein and his contribution to the field of prevention and intervention and his humanistic approach to treating children and their families. We hope these guides will enhance the ability of motivated, skilled, and enthusiastic practitioners to put his effective methods to work.

MARK AMENDOLA   ROBERT OLIVER
PERSEUS HOUSE, INC.   PERSEUS HOUSE EDUCATION AND TREATMENT
ERIE, PENNSYLVANIA   ALTERNATIVES
ERIE, PENNSYLVANIA

Acknowledgments

Acknowledgments must first go to Mark Amendola and Bob Oliver for their development and leadership in bringing the Prepare Curriculum Implentation Guide idea to life, and to Karen Steiner, Judy Parkinson, and the rest of the Research Press team, who have been supportive, encouraging, and collaborative.

Of course, we are deeply grateful to Arnold P. Goldstein, who wrote the two editions of the *Prepare Curriculum,* published in 1988 and 1999. Our thanks also go to John C. Gibbs and Granville Bud Potter, who with Arnold Goldstein created the EQUIP program, which must be acknowledged as an important milestone in the development of Goldstein's accomplishments.

As authors, we are grateful for the work of Larry Brentro, Martin Brokenleg, and Steve Van Bockern of the Circle of Courage and Reclaiming Children and Youth International. Their philosophy for all youth to experience belonging, mastery, independence, and generosity has been influential in the development of strategies incorporated into the approaches of this Problem-Solving Training guide.

We appreciate the contributions to the Prepare Curriculum by dozens of Dr. Goldstein's thesis and dissertation advisees, colleagues from his university, and many other unnamed contributors to his work. We have certainly benefited from the similar experience of colleagues and friends associated with what we have come to call "Arnie's Army."

And finally, for the inspiration of Ellen McGinnis, Sara Salmon, Eva Feindler, Bengt Daleflod, and Borge Strømgren, we are also very grateful.

Introduction: About the Prepare Curriculum

—Clive R. Hollin

The Prepare Curriculum, developed and later revised by Arnold Goldstein (Goldstein, 1988, 1999), takes a psychoeducational approach to working with young people who experience difficulties with interpersonal relationships and prosocial behavior. Prepare is designed to provide practitioners, teachers, and therapists with a series of coordinated psychoeducational courses explicitly developed to teach an array of prosocial psychological competencies to adolescents and younger children who are deficient in such competencies. As Goldstein notes in the introduction to the 1999 edition:

> It seeks to teach empathy, which is interwoven into many of the modules, cooperation to the uncooperative, problem solving to those with inadequate decision-making skills, negotiating skills to the stubborn, anger control to the impulsive, altruism to the egocentric, group process to the isolated, stress management to the anxious, and social perceptiveness to the socially confused. (p. 1)

Prepare has its practice roots firmly in the tradition of skills training (Hollin & Trower, 1986a, 1986b) and, allied to social learning theory, to the application of cognitive-behavioral therapy to adolescent problems (Goldstein, Nensén, Daleflod, & Kalt, 2004). The techniques used in Prepare—including modeling, cognitive skills training, emotional control training, and problem-solving training—are traditional components of cognitive-behavioral interventions used to bring about change in cognitive, emotional, and behavioral skills. As these behavior change techniques are used in unison to bring about a range of changes, Prepare is an example of a multimodal program. A multimodal approach is in sympathy with the view that to bring about change in people's lives it is necessary to attend to multiple factors (Nietzel, Hasemann, & Lynam, 1999; Tate, Reppucci, & Mulvey, 1995). The effectiveness of multimodal programs such as Prepare with young people is supported in the literature (Hatcher & Hollin, 2005; Hollin & Palmer, 2006b; Lipsey & Wilson, 1998).

Clive R. Hollin is Professor of Psychology at the University of Leicester in England. His research lies in the interface between psychology and criminology, particularly with regard to the management and treatment of offenders.

Prepare also has foundations in an earlier program, described in the book *Aggression Replacement Training* (ART; Glick & Gibbs, 2011; Goldstein & Glick, 1987; Goldstein, Glick, & Gibbs, 1998). ART encompasses a tripartite approach, employing the three behavior change techniques of Skillstreaming, Anger Control Training, and Moral Reasoning. Whereas ART was designed for use with highly aggressive young people, Prepare incorporates a considerably wider spectrum of techniques aimed at the larger numbers of young people who have difficulties with prosocial behavior. Thus, Prepare may be used with young people who are moderately aggressive or who are socially isolated and withdrawn.

PREPARE COURSES

The Prepare Curriculum consists of 10 courses that focus on the behaviors, cognitions, and emotions related to prosocial interaction. These courses target three areas: aggression, stress, and prejudice reduction. As shown in Table 1, the Prepare courses for aggression include the three original ART courses (Skillstreaming, Anger Control Training, and Moral Reasoning Training), with an additional course on Situational Perception Training. The courses that focus on stress are Recruiting Supportive Models, Stress Management Training, and Problem-Solving Training. Finally, the courses for prejudice reduction include Cooperation Training, Empathy Training, and Understanding and Using Groups.

THEORETICAL BACKGROUND

Goldstein (1999) describes how several theoretical perspectives influenced both the original design and later refinement of the Prepare Curriculum. Acknowledging the importance of psychodynamic and client-centered theory approaches to helping people change, Goldstein is clear that social learning theory and skills training are the key influences of Prepare. Simply, social learning theory seeks to understand the complex interactions among an individual's thoughts, emotions, and actions within a given social context (Bandura, 1977b, 1986). In terms of practice, social learning theory is perhaps most closely allied with cognitive-behavioral methods, including skills training, traditionally much used with antisocial young people (Hollin, 1990). Furthermore, Goldstein's view of interpersonal problems is very much in sympathy with a social learning approach. For example, Goldstein (1994) described three levels in the physical ecology of aggression, all incorporating various levels of a person-environment interaction: "Macrolevel" refers to the analysis of aggression at a national or regional level, "mesolevel" to violence at the neighborhood level, and "microlevel" to violence found in settings such as the home and on the street.

The application of social learning theory is axiomatic with an approach to practice that sees the possibilities for change in both the social environment and the individual. At the level of work with the individual young person, practice is concerned with multimodal change that encompasses the individual's thoughts, emotions, and actions. As is evident from the curriculum, Prepare adopts a multimodal approach to change, with a clear emphasis on skills development. Indeed, the approach to skills development within Prepare is in keeping with the original social skills model described by Argyle and Kendon (1967). Argyle and Kendon described socially skilled behavior as consisting of three related components—namely, social perception, social cognition, and social performance. Social perception skills are evident in the ability to perceive and

Table 1: Grouping of Prepare Curriculum Courses

	AGGRESSION	STRESS	PREJUDICE REDUCTION
Behavioral	Skillstreaming Situational Perception Training	Recruiting Supportive Models	Cooperation Training
Emotional	Anger Control Training	Stress Management Training	Empathy Training
Cognitive	Moral Reasoning Training	Problem-Solving Training	Understanding and Using Groups

understand verbal and nonverbal social cues. Social cognition, as used in this context, is broadly analogous to social information processing and social problem solving. Social performance refers to the individual's own mastery of verbal and nonverbal behaviors. The socially able person will be able to use all three components of social skills in an integrated manner to function effectively with other people.

Newer research on brain development and the neurosciences also has had an impact on our understanding of social cognition and perception. Goleman's (2005) work with social intelligence assists with the development of best practice for social skills training. His discussion of the brain's design to be sociable provides a neural bridge that impacts learning. The more strongly we are connected with someone emotionally, the greater the potential for lasting change. So, just as prosocial relationships affect neurological connectedness by impacting the size and shape of synapses, negative relationships can have a toxic effect. These newer developments have important implications for evidence-based programs.

RESEARCH OVERVIEW

If the theoretical and practical underpinnings of the Prepare Curriculum are sound, what is the evidence to suggest that some young people have specific difficulties in the areas addressed within Prepare? A body of research suggests that the three major targets of aggression, stress, and prejudice reduction within Prepare are aimed at appropriate aspects of young people's functioning with respect to their prosocial behavior. An overview of this evidence in support of the behavioral, emotional, or cognitive change for these three major targets is next provided.

Behavior Focus

Situational Perception Training

Situational Perception Training is designed to develop the young person's social competence in applying the social skills learned in Skillstreaming. The purpose of Situational Perception Training is to show that in a social interaction, as well as in the other person's actions, situational, contextual factors are important to consider. The skill of accurately perceiving a person-situation interaction, rather than assuming, say, that another person is deliberately hostile, is an important element in developing social competence.

The skills to recognize, understand, and interpret situational cues are an essential part of effective interpersonal behavior (Argyle, 1983). However, some young people with interpersonal difficulties, including aggression, may have difficulties in both the selection and interpretation of social cues (e.g., Akhtar & Bradley, 1991; Lipton, McDonel, & McFall, 1987; Lösel, Bliesener, & Bender, 2007; McCown, Johnson, & Austin, 1986). The misperception of social cues may lead to misattribution of the actions of other people as hostile or threatening (Crick & Dodge, 1996). Misperception of the other people's intent will, in turn, influence the way in which the young person deals with a given social encounter. Thus, Situational Perception Training is intended to develop the young person's skills in accurately detecting and understanding the verbal and nonverbal nuances that are present within a social interaction. Situational Perception Training therefore focuses on the setting in which the interaction takes place, the purpose of the interaction, and the social relationship between those involved (Brown & Fraser, 1979). The learning that takes place with perception training augments the skill development associated with Skillstreaming, enhancing the closeness of the match between Prepare and the original social skills model (Argyle & Kendon, 1967). The closeness of the match between theory and practice increases the likelihood of a successful outcome. The expansion of the Prepare course is called Social Perception Training to reflect its more comprehensive nature.

Skillstreaming

Skillstreaming is the development of skills, through the use of the techniques of modeling, instruction, practice, and feedback, to allow the young person to replace destructive behaviors with more constructive, prosocial alternative behaviors. Spence (1981a, 1981b) compared the social performance skills of young male offenders with those of matched nondelinquent controls. Spence reported differences in levels of nonverbal skills such that the delinquents were rated less favorably in terms of social skill, social anxiety, and employability. Ample evidence shows that skills training—incorporating modeling, role-play, and instructional feedback—can increase young people's social skills (Hollin & Palmer, 2001).

Recruiting Supportive Models

The Prepare course on recruiting supportive models aims to help young people to recognize, recruit, and maintain a prosocial support group. Goldstein's (2004a, 2004b) evaluation of the three original ART courses concludes that participation of the individual's significant other(s) in the courses is likely further to improve their success. The extension of the Prepare course Recruiting Supportive Models is *Family TIES* (Teaching in Essential Skills; Calame & Parker, 2013), which incorporates the family as the main support system.

Cooperation Training

The Prepare Curriculum originally involved two broad approaches designed to increase cooperative behavior: cooperative learning and cooperative gaming. The course offered numerous exercises, organized by age group, to enhance prosocial and achievement behaviors.

Johnson, Johnson, and Stanne (2000) conducted a meta-analysis of 158 studies of cooperative learning strategies. They reported that the research clearly presents evidence that cooperative learning produces positive achievement results. Brown and Ciuffetelli (2009) highlight five basic and essential elements of cooperative learning: (a) positive interdependence; (b) face-to-face promotive interaction; (c) individual accountability; (d) social skills; and (e) group processing. Other positive outcomes of cooperative learning are increased self- and co-regulation leading to better problem solving (DiDonato, 2013).

Movement training utilizes cooperative activities and games to further enhance learning and retention of the skills taught to youth who participate in the Prepare series groups. Movement training incorporates physical movements that will stimulate and prepare the brain for learning. Ratey (2008) describes movement and exercise as "Miracle-Gro" for the brain, greatly enhancing self-awareness, self-esteem, and social skills. The typical child's attention span is reported to be three to five minutes per year of the child's age (Schmitt, 1999). A decrease in attention is exacerbated by inactivity. Movement can be used before, during, and after group participation to increase attention and enhance learning.

Emotion Focus

Anger Control Training

Anger Control Training involves the application of anger management techniques to previously assessed triggers for the young person's anger. Thus, this course aims to improve the young person's control over anger by developing a self-awareness of internal anger cues, increasing self-instructional skills, facilitating the use of coping strategies and social problem-solving skills, and increasing social skills.

Anger, particularly dysfunctional anger, is the emotional state most frequently associated with aggressive behavior (Davey, Day, & Howells, 2005), although not all violent conduct is associated with anger. Anger is seen to be dysfunctional when it has a negative consequence either for the individual, as seen with poor physical and mental health, or for other people (Swaffer & Hollin, 2000, 2001). The most influential theory of anger was formulated by Novaco (1975, 2007), in which anger is understood to be a subjective emotional state involving both physiological and cognitive activity, but clearly related to environmental circumstances.

Following Novaco's theory, the experience of anger is triggered by some environmental event, typically the individual's perception of the words and actions of another person. Novaco and Welsh (1989) identified various styles of perception and information processing that are typical of individuals who are prone to anger. These styles include the tendency to see hostility and provocation in the words and actions of other people and to make attribution errors in perceiving one's own behavior as situationally determined by the behavior of others, as explained by their negative personality.

The individual's misperception of a situation may prompt distinct patterns of physiological and cognitive arousal. The physiological correlates of anger are typically a rise in body temperature, perspiration and muscular tension and increased cardiovascular activity. The cognitive processes begin with the individual's labeling the emotional state as anger and then continue with the intensification of the information-processing biases as the situation unfolds. Finally, the shift from anger to violent behavior is related to the disinhibition of internal control through, for example, high levels of physiological arousal or the effects of drugs.

Anger control training in various forms is now widely used across a range of populations, including young people, with a strong supporting research base (Hollin & Bloxsom, 2007).

Stress Management Training

Stress Management Training recognizes that stressful life events may have negative effects on young people. The development of stress management skills is achieved through the application of such techniques as progressive relaxation training, meditation, controlled breathing, and physical exercise, as well as through reflective exercises looking at how to deal with personally stressful life events.

As is the case with anger, stress and anxiety can be both functional and dysfunctional. Childhood and adolescence present a myriad of changing life events that are naturally stressful for the developing young adult (Frydenberg, 1997). The Stress Management Training course in Prepare aims to help individuals regulate their stress so that it does not affect their ability to use their prosocial skills effectively. The tendency of adolescents to be peer-conscious can make some young people particularly susceptible to social stressors. The experience of stress, in turn, may interfere with the young person's ability to perform well in some social interactions.

Empathy Training

Empathy Training encourages young people to reflect upon other people's feelings and to increase awareness that the feelings of other people may be different from their own. The basis of this training lies in the view that if an individual has the capacity to empathize, then he or she is less likely to misperceive hostile intent in the actions of other people. Increasing empathy may reduce the likelihood of the young person's being aggressive toward others.

The ability to appreciate another person's emotional state is a key component of prosocial behavior. Goldstein (2004a) suggests that empathy and aggression cannot coexist, given that an empathic state will inhibit an aggressive one. It follows, therefore, that increasing a young person's capacity for empathy may reduce the likelihood of the young person's displaying hostility and aggression to other people.

A distinction is made in the literature between affective empathy and cognitive empathy. Affective empathy is seen in the emotions we experience in response to another person's situation. Cognitive empathy is our intellectual understanding of how another person feels. The research literature suggests a relationship between low empathy and offending (Miller & Eisenberg, 1988). Jolliffe and Farrington (2007) found a relationship between low cognitive and affective empathy and offending. However, Jolliffe and Farrington also reported that the relationship was more consistent in males than in females and was moderated by the level of the young person's intelligence and socioeconomic status. These studies provide support for the inclusion of empathy training as an integral part of Prepare.

Cognitive Focus

Moral Reasoning Training

Moral Reasoning Training is intended to resolve maturational delays with respect to moral reasoning and any associated egocentric bias. This aspect of Prepare includes enhancement of moral reasoning, alongside social perspective-taking skills, using the techniques of self-instruction training, social problem-solving skills training, and guided peer group social decision making.

The importance of moral development in socialization is made clear in several influential theories (Kohlberg, 1978; Piaget, 1932). In particular, Kohlberg's theory is concerned with the development of antisocial behavior. Kohlberg, like Piaget, argues that as the child grows older moral reasoning follows a developmental sequence in line with the child's age. Kohlberg describes three levels of moral development, with two stages at each level. At the lower stages, moral reasoning is concrete in orientation. Reasoning becomes more abstract at the higher stages, involving concepts such as justice and rights.

Kohlberg suggests that antisocial behavior is associated with a delay in the development of moral reasoning that results in weak internal control over behavior. The generally accepted position, reinforced by the major reviews, is that delinquents typically show immature, hedonistic, and self-centered moral functioning when compared with their nondelinquent peers (Nelson, Smith, & Dodd, 1990; Palmer, 2003; Stams et al., 2006).

However, as Gibbs (1993) points out, moral reasoning should be considered alongside other aspects of cognition, particularly social information processing, particularly with regard to cognitive distortions (Gibbs, 1993; Goldstein et al., 1998). Cognitive distortions directly support the attitudes consistent with sociomoral developmental delay and reduce cognitive dissonance. Thus, an example of self-centered moral reasoning would be "If I want it, I take it." Gibbs terms this type of reasoning a primary distortion. Primary distortions are sustained by secondary distortions: Secondary distortions supporting "I want it, I take it" might be blaming victims for the offense or biased interpretations of one's own behavior. The successful use of Moral Reasoning Training with aggressive populations has been reported in the literature (Gibbs, 1996; Gibbs, Potter, & Goldstein, 1995).

Problem-Solving Training

Problem-Solving Training is included because the young person's problem-solving ability affects how successfully he or she may learn and apply other Prepare skills in real life. Thus, Problem-Solving Training helps the young person develop skills and abilities in defining a problem, identifying potential solutions, selecting the optimal solution, and evaluating the effectiveness of the chosen strategy.

Following perception and understanding of other people's behavior, the young person must choose a suitable behavioral response. The process of decision making in the context of a social interaction requires the young person to problem-solve—that is, to think of potential courses of action, to consider the alternatives and their likely consequences, and to plan toward accomplishing the intended outcome (McGuire, 2005). Some young people may experience difficulties in social problem solving. For example, both female and male young offenders typically employ a more limited range of alternatives to solve interpersonal problems and rely more on verbal and physical aggression than do nondelinquents (Hollin & Palmer, 2006a; Palmer & Hollin, 1999; Ward & McFall, 1986). A body of research that supports the effectiveness of problem-solving training with young people (Lösel & Beelmann, 2005).

Understanding and Using Groups

As Goldstein (1999) points out, "Group processes are an exceedingly important influence upon the daily lives of many adolescents and younger children" (p. 737). The Prepare course on groups encompasses discussion of the nature, dynamics, problems, and opportunities in groups. In addition to providing a conceptual context, the course describes numerous experiential opportunities to help youth understand and use groups to prosocial advantage.

Groups develop through four stages: forming, storming, norming, and performing (Tuckman, 1965; Tuckman & Jensen, 1977). At the forming stage, even though members may not know each other very well, it is important to set boundaries and clear parameters for the operation of the group. Safety is clearly the priority, for if there is no safety, there is no growth. When groups are forming, the facilitators provide support and guidance to establish a climate of psychological and emotional safety. Facilitators also should be keenly aware of any negative influences in the group and any bullying behavior that may be unsafe and/or counterproductive to the goals of the group.

In the second stage, storming, members will test limits to determine whether the group is safe. Individuals may push boundaries and break commitments that they made in the initial session. It is the role and responsibility of facilitators to correct and/or address such behavior. If facilitators and members fail to enforce and comply with norms, the safety and growth of the group will be impaired.

During the third stage, norming, relationships develop, and, as trust increases, members become more willing to take risks (Amidon, Roth, & Greenberg, 1991). The group should begin to work together to problem-solve, resolve conflict, and share personal values. Because adolescents are constantly attempting to discover their identity and role in relation to others, their interaction with one another, if positive, will assist in crystallizing this identity and role. Also during this stage, we begin to see prosocial coaching occur from peer to peer. When this transpires, our experience has been that group members begin to internalize and learn skills at a deeper level.

In the more advanced performing stage, we begin to see the group functioning at its highest level. Facilitators' roles are to ease transitions and provide support to the group. Trust is at its highest level, and we also see peers exhibit empathic responses to one another. During this time, higher risk engagement and activities are possible, with facilitators remaining intensely aware of any negative environmental influences.

When delivered with fidelity, psychoeducational groups can help increase self-awareness, build healthy relationships, and improve interpersonal connections. This therapeutic environment also assists with competency development and skill building, which encourage appropriate expression of emotion, minimizing the negative and maximizing the positive. Processing group experiences also increases self-awareness, self-disclosure, healthy boundaries, and improved relationships (Thompson & White, 2010).

We have found through our practical application of the Prepare Curriculum that the development of group process is impacted by the skill level of the facilitator and engagement of the participants. When groups are functioning at their highest level, there is mutual benefit to a larger number of participants, and we see proficient levels of skill demonstrated in real-life situations.

CONCLUSION

Some young people experience difficulties as they grow older in developing and using prosocial skills. These difficulties are obviously not a characteristic of all young people, who form a heterogeneous population with an accordingly broad span of social ability (Veneziano & Veneziano, 1988). Nonetheless, for those young people who do experience such problems, attention to the development of prosocial competencies may help in reducing antisocial behavior and moving them toward a more rewarding social life.

PART 1
Introduction to Problem-Solving Training

INTRODUCTION

The scientific method, in its essence, is a problem-solving process. Science has put effort into creating logical ways of solving scientific problems, and it is clear that a refinement of the way we process problems can also be meaningful in everyday life. *Problem solving, decision making,* and *problem-solving training* are terms for practice used in a variety of settings and with a variety of issues, including depression (Nezu & Perri, 1989), family conflicts (Foster, Prinz, & O'Leary, 1983), schizophrenia (Ucok et al., 2006), prevention of early aggression (Dodsworth, 2002), and educational difficulties (Shure, 2001).

Over the past several decades, many studies have investigated the relationship between social problem solving and depression. Dobson and Dobson (1981) examined depressed versus nondepressed college students. Depressed students evidenced various problem-solving deficits and a conservative problem-solving style. In their 1987 study, Nezu and Ronan found that depressed college students performed worse on problem-solving tasks when compared with their counterparts who were not depressed. Since then, Goodman, Gravitt, and Kaslow (1995) concluded that children who find less effective alternative solutions in problem solving also report higher levels of depressive symptoms. Of even greater concern is the fact that problem-solving deficits increase hopelessness, which in turn increases suicidal ideation (Nezu, Wilkins, & Maguth-Nezu, 2004).

The goal of parents and educators is to prepare children and youth to become responsible citizens. We can accomplish this by strengthening their ability to think clearly and carefully, even under stress. Howard Gardner (1993) encourages openness to developing all aspects of intelligence, including scientific, artistic, and kinesthetic intelligence, as well as interpersonal and intrapersonal competencies. Both these personal competencies are important components of problem solving.

With respect to her own problem-solving program, Shure (2001) has also found that

> within a wide range of IQ . . . gains in Interpersonal Cognitive Problem Solving are linked with improvements in interpersonal behaviors, which are in turn linked with gains in objectively measured math and reading levels. It appears that once behaviors mediated through ICPS [Interpersonal Cognitive Problem Solving] skills improve, youngsters can absorb the task oriented demands of the classroom and subsequently do better in school. (p. 3)

The structure of problem-solving training in clinical settings varies and focuses on both interpersonal problem solving and impersonal problem solving. Impersonal problem solving is concerned with solving rational, usually nonemotional problems, whereas the concern of interpersonal problem solving is to avoid or resolve problems that occur in relationships with others. Interpersonal problem solving is thus normally part of an attempt to enhance social competency, either as a separate program or as a component of a broader multimodal program, such as the Prepare Curriculum (Goldstein, 1999).

Problem-solving ability is, first of all, an immensely important set of skills that assist people of all ages in navigating difficult situations. With youth as our focus in this volume, we clearly see that the conflict, confusion, and difficult choices young people face daily create high levels of stress. To have in place a useful strategy for dealing with this ongoing conflict is essential for problem resolution. It is particularly helpful when guiding and helping challenged youth whose problem-solving skills are still in the stages of development.

It is important to make a distinction between the concepts of problem solving and solution implementation. *Problem solving* refers to the process of finding solutions to specific problems, whereas *solution implementation* refers to the process of putting into practice proposed solutions in actual problem situations (D'Zurilla, Nezu, & Maydeu-Olivares, 2004). While problem solving is considered to be a general skill that can be used across different settings, solution implementation is about the variety of optional skills that can be implemented depending on the situation and actual problem. Thus people can know how to solve problems while lacking solution implementation skills and vice versa. Therefore, problem solving should be viewed in the context of this discussion as both skill and meta-skill, and it is an advantage to combine the training of problem-solving skills with the training of social skills.

Problem-solving training has proven successful in reducing antisocial behavior both as a single modal program (Friendship, Blund, Erikson, Travers, & Thornton, 2003) and in combination with anger control training (Sukhodolsky, Golub, Stone, & Orban, 2005) and social skills training (Tsang & Pearson, 2001). In his work with fifth- and sixth-grade children, Crutchfield (1969) designed problem-solving skills that identified the boundary conditions of the problem, put facts in order, discriminated relevant from irrelevant facts, recognized gaps in available information, and specified what other information was needed to fill these gaps.

In a problem-solving program for individuals with schizophrenia (Bellack, Mueser, Gingerich, & Agresta, 1997), for example, the following steps are included:

1. Define the problem.
2. Use brainstorming to generate possible solutions for the problem.
3. Identify the advantages and disadvantages of each possible solution.
4. Select the "best" solution or combination of solutions.
5. Plan how to carry out the solution(s).
6. Follow up the plan at a later time.

Because problem-solving and solution implementation skills are required for effective functioning or social competence, it is often necessary to combine training in problem-solving skills with training in other social and behavioral performance skills to maximize positive outcomes (McFall, 1982). In many social skills programs, problem-solving training has been included as one or more specific skills. Problem solving is an element that figures into many of the Prepare Curriculum courses: (a) in deciding which Skillstreaming skills to select; (b) in Social Perception Training, when choosing the appropriate context in which to use the skill; (c) in matching arousal reduction techniques to particular provocations in Anger Control Training; (d) in evaluating alternative solutions in Moral Reasoning Training dilemmas; (e) in determining what, where, when, and how long to use a Stress Management Training technique; (f) in working as a group to complete the activities of Cooperation Training; and (g) in solving many problems of leadership, clique formation, and peer pressure, as described in Understanding and Using Groups (Goldstein, 1999).

The goal of Problem-Solving Training as presented here is to teach youth of all ages a way to navigate through and/or solve their own problems. Thus, the main purpose in training is not to help the participants solve their actual problems, but rather to give them a structured method or process to follow that can help them when solving the problems they will face in their future lives.

Important general principles of training are as follows:

1. Participants should learn the prerequisite language and conceptual skills.

2. New concepts should be taught with words already familiar to the youth.

3. The content of the program should center on personal and interpersonal themes, with less focus on impersonal problems.

4. Emphasis should be on conceptual learning and understanding (e.g., on the concept and process of negotiating and not on learning words and their definitions).

5. A main goal is to teach youth the skill of creating alternative solutions and evaluating them on the basis of consequences. (For example, if a youth suggests that one solution to a problem would be to "hit him," the facilitator should respond, "That's one idea. Do you have a different solution? Can you think of a more prosocial alternative?")

6. Youth should come up with their own ideas and be encouraged to offer them in the context of the problem situation.

MODELS OF PROBLEM-SOLVING TRAINING

A specific program in problem-solving training is normally comprehensive and delves deeply into cognitive obstacles or thinking patterns that can hinder decision making. In the Prepare Curriculum, Goldstein's problem-solving training methods are based generally on the work of D'Zurilla and Goldfried (1971) and the I Can Problem Solve (ICPS) method, first described by Spivack, Platt, and Shure (1976).

Problem Solving in Cognitive-Behavioral Treatment

The program probably most often integrated into cognitive-behavioral treatment (McMurran, 2006) is based on the work of D'Zurilla and Goldfried (1971), more recently described by Chang, D'Zurilla, and Sanna (2004). Briefly, the program includes the following steps.

Problem Orientation

Problem orientation concerns a set of orienting responses that includes beliefs, assumptions, appraisals, and expectations concerning life's problems and one's own general problem-solving ability (Nezu & Perri, 1989).

Problem Definition and Formulation

Gathering information. In gathering information, one distinguishes between task information and behavioral information, splitting the problem into smaller problems, and uses techniques for making the problem more concrete (in which situation, what is and is not wrong, when it is and is not better, etc.).

Understanding the problem. One understands a problem by answering relevant questions such as (a) What present conditions are unacceptable? (b) What changes or additions are demanded or desired? (c) What obstacle(s) are preventing the person from meeting the demand?

Setting the goal. Setting the goal involves developing a goal that is concrete, measurable, and realistic.

Generating Alternative Solutions

Generating alternative solutions entails (a) taking into consideration that the more available solutions the better and (b) creating a wide variety of solutions without judging their value.

Decision Making

Decision making involves considering three questions: (a) What hinders you in implementing the different solutions? (b) What do you think will happen if you implement the specific solution? and (c) Which solution should you choose?

Solution Implementation and Verification

Solution implementation and verification involve carrying out the chosen solution, assessing the actual outcome, and making any corrections necessary.

෨෬

When using this model, we have experienced that problems can be resolved or reduced even in the initial part of the process. Splitting problems into different parts sometimes makes them seem less overwhelming. Setting goals for progress also can make the solution more realistic and less problematic.

Interpersonal Cognitive Problem Solving

Interpersonal Cognitive Problem Solving (ICPS) was originally developed by Spivack et al. (1976) and extended by Shure (2001). In its earliest phase, ICPS training was directed primarily toward young children. Spivack and Shure (1974) communicate why, in the context of aggressive behavior, they view problem-solving skills worth teaching:

> What might an adult say to a preschool child who hits another or grabs a toy or cries? One possible response is "Kevin, I know you feel angry at Paul, but I can't let you hit him." Another is "Paul doesn't like to be hit." Sean snatches a truck from Robert and the adult asks him why he has taken the truck. "I want it" is the answer. "Wait until Robert is finished and then you can play with it," says the adult. . . . In handling such behaviors as hitting and grabbing, many teachers and parents of young children demand that the behavior stop "because I said so." They often explain why the behavior is unacceptable.
>
> We believe that such techniques have serious limitations if one's goal is to help children develop effective ways of handling personal and interpersonal problems. First, the adult is too often thinking for the child. The child is told they should wait their turn or stay away from another child or not hit. . . . The child neither solves his problem nor discovers a solution on his own. Second, the adult in attempting to help a child

often assumes that the child has a real understanding of the language of emotions ("I know you feel angry") or of negation ("but I can't let you hit") or of causal relationships ("because you might hurt him").

Finally, solving a problem for a child does little to help him feel good about himself. He is simply told what he can or cannot do, even though the reasons might be explained and the solution might work in that particular instance. He does not experience the mastery that emerges when one has solved a problem. He may feel protected, but not competent. (pp. ix–x)

It is from this rationale that the ICPS program emerged. The program was designed to teach children (and later, adolescents and adults) *how* to think, not *what* to think—the problem-solving process, not problem solutions. From this viewpoint emerged the following ICPS principles or guidelines.

Alternative Solution Thinking

One of the basic goals of problem-solving training is to expand the capacity for alternative solutions. Spivack and colleagues (1976) observed that if someone has only one or two solutions to a problem, the chance for success is less than if he or she can come up with different solutions if the first fails.

Consequential Thinking

The second ICPS skill is defined as the ability to consider how one's actions may affect other people and oneself. To enhance this ability, a facilitator can follow a suggestion from participants with questions like "What might happen next?" "How will this make Mary feel?" "What will happen in the short run?" and "What will happen in the long run?"

Causal Thinking

Causal, or cause-and-effect, thinking is the ability to relate one event to another. A low ability to engage in causal thinking makes it difficult to react logically and appropriately to the behavior of others, and low causal thinking may result in misunderstanding others' behavior as threatening. A person capable of causal thinking is capable of suspending judgment until sufficient factual information is available (Muuss, 1960).

Interpersonal Sensitivity

This skill reflects the ability to be aware that an interpersonal problem in fact exists. If a person who is involved with a conflict recognizes only his or her own problem and not the problem of others or is acting without considering that his or her own actions can generate problems for others, conflicts have a tendency to increase.

Means-End Thinking

Means-end thinking is careful, step-by-step planning to reach a given goal. Training in this type of thinking involves forestalling potential obstacles that may occur when planning, including choosing the right time and other means to reach the goal. Spivack (Spivack et al., 1976) exemplifies this concept by describing a boy who has just moved into a new apartment. He considers visiting the boy next door (goal), but he doesn't know him and so doesn't think the boy will let him in (obstacle). The first boy can call and explain that he has just moved in (means), and the second boy will probably say OK and let him in. We can then look at the situation from the second boy's perspective: He wants to meet the first boy (goal), but his mother will be mad if the first boy comes to visit at dinnertime (obstacle). The solution to reach the goal will be to propose that the first boy come to visit after dinner (means).

Perspective Taking

Perspective-taking skills reflect the extent to which an individual recognizes and integrates the fact that different people have different motives and viewpoints and thus may respond differently in any given situation. Perspective taking is closely linked to the concept of empathy.

SESSION OVERVIEW

The Problem-Solving Training sessions take into account the theoretical base laid out by Goldstein, D'Zurilla, Nezu, Spivack, Shure, and others.

Session 1: Overview of Problem Solving

In this session, an overview of the program is delivered and a commitment to participate is elicited from the youth. In real life, problem solving rarely occurs according to the neatly ordered steps laid out in the theory. Every step in problem solving may, in itself, be a process. Each participant understands the step in his or her own way, and for some this understanding may be more complex than for others.

For example, in defining a problem, one youth may get to the crux of the matter much more quickly than another. That participant may be readily aware of physical cues and sensitive to his or her own feelings. Another participant may be completely out of touch with such cues and need to go through a mental checklist. The same holds true for gathering information. A participant who has difficulty reading others' body language will need many more strategies than will a more perceptive youth.

The problem-solving steps may change in order, may interact with one another, and/or overlap. Central to the problem-solving approach is the goal of teaching youth a way of organizing these problem-solving procedures, as opposed to merely describing the actual problem-solving process (D'Zurilla & Goldfried, 1971).

The session also includes discussion with participants about what a problem is. D'Zurilla et al. (2004) explain:

> A *problem* (or problematic situation) is defined as any life situation or task (present or anticipated) that demands a response for adaptive functioning but no effective response is immediately apparent or available to the person or people confronted with a situation because of the presence of one or more obstacles. (p. 12)

Session 2: Barriers to Problem Solving—Cognitive Distortions/ Thinking Errors

The goal of problem solving is to decide what the best course of action is when one is presented with an obstacle. Often, those who have problem-solving deficits engage in cognitive distortions, or thinking errors, to justify their behaviors. To solve problems effectively, participants must recognize and correct thinking errors such as being self-centered, blaming others, assuming the worst, expecting hostility, and minimizing. It is critical that they understand which part of the problem belongs to them because, without any ownership, there can be no self-generated solution.

Thinking errors are present everywhere in life, and we recognize that we all engage in such thinking to some degree. We may think of times we have lied or misrepresented a situation. We may recall, with some embarrassment, an occasion when we have let our temper get the best of us or an isolated instance of taking something that did not belong to us. Such behavior doesn't automatically place us on the self-destructive and/or antisocial end of the continuum. However, eliminating wrong thinking patterns and learning new ones is crucial to problem solving, and genuine self-criticism is absolutely essential to the change process. It is important to help participants recognize that thinking errors are a barrier to problem solving, counteract their conviction that improvement is not necessary, and promote understanding that thinking errors can be harmful to themselves and others.

Session 3: Problem Signs/Stop and Think

As early as 1950, Dollard and Miller recognized that the first step in the simplest type of reasoning is to stop and think. They claimed that if a person responds immediately when confronted with a problematic situation, the individual may not recognize important cues that can help the person select the most appropriate and effective course of action.

This is the time for participants to recognize problem signs and learn to stop and think. They realize that problems are normal, begin to understand that they must resist behaving impulsively, and learn to tap into their own problem-solving abilities. In our experience, it is valuable to point out that the first sign of a problem is usually a change in mood or feelings. Having participants become sensitive to these physical and emotional cues can help them know when it is time to stop and think. One needs to be conscious of a shift in emotion when encountering a situation. If a shift occurs, one must consider whether this is indeed a problematic situation. It is also important for participants to develop a personal protocol prior to making any overt response. This can reduce the tendency either to react automatically (perhaps inappropriately) or to do nothing, which may worsen the problem and leave it unresolved through avoidance.

Session 4: Problem Identification

It is important for youth to realize that one can't solve a problem that is too big, too confused, or too vague. There also may be times when the problem does not stand alone but is rather a cluster of problems that must be taken on one at a time. Once an individual recognizes that he or she is facing a problem situation and avoids an automatic response, he or she must then proceed to use the elements of problem identification. These are (a) defining the problem and (b) breaking down elements of the situation by separating irrelevant information, primary goals, and major obstacles. For an effective process to occur, the problem solver must be encouraged to be clear and specific. Consequently, the individual is obliged to look at and make relevant what may have seemed irrelevant at first. The use of means-end thinking—or thinking about potential obstacles, sequences of events, and time or timing—also may be pertinent

(D'Zurilla & Goldfried, 1971; Shure, 2001). Problem identification prescribes that means-end thinking must be considered when defining the elements of the problem and setting a goal to resolve it.

In general, problems result from issues of control, and differences between people's personal goals. Often youth will fall into the trap of solving problems by trying to manipulate others into doing what they want. According to D'Zurilla, problem-solving training may be conceived as a form of self-control or independence training. It is, therefore, much more productive to focus on problems using self-control and asking oneself "What can I do to improve this situation?" Youth also have a tendency to put their needs and desires before those of others, which may turn a problem into a power issue. Our ultimate goal is to strengthen prosocial skills for the betterment of interpersonal relationships. Facilitators must stress understanding and acknowledgement of the differences in people's personal goals. The focus needs to shift from attempting to manipulate others' goals to acceptance of and respect for the differences. Problems may also reflect a search for something or someone or be caused by uncertainty or unclear expectations.

Session 5: Gathering Information (Own and Others' Perspective)

As Muuss (1960) states, "High causally oriented subjects show more security and less anxiety" (p. 128). Our goal, therefore, is to promote causal thinking in order to decrease the stress level that often accompanies a problem. To avoid making impulsive or misinformed decisions, one must carefully examine all facets of the problem and seek as much information as possible (D'Zurilla & Goldfried, 1971). This holds true not only when the problem is new or unfamiliar but also when it occurs frequently.

Good decisions are based on gathering and considering as many perspectives as possible. Youth are encouraged to examine the perspectives of other people in order to gain a more well-rounded insight into the problem. When gathering perspectives, participants should learn to separate fact from opinion. Doing so may involve differentiating between reality and egocentric bias, challenging pessimistic views of others or themselves, and accepting responsibility. We encourage the problem-solver to put the problem into words: In your own words, what is the problem? Have you felt this way before? What was happening? Try to say, "I feel ____because_____" or "When _____happens, I feel_____."

These questions help the problem-solver gather information about his or her own feelings and perspectives and also highlight similar provocative situations that have, in the past, led to similar feelings (Elias & Tobias, 1996).

Session 6: Brainstorming Alternatives

Subsequent to gathering information from one's own and others' perspectives is the task of generating possible solutions to the problem. Brainstorming is the means to answer the question "What do *I* need to change?" to solve the problem.

D'Zurilla and Goldfried (1971) expand on brainstorming, citing four basic rules:

1. Criticism is ruled out: withhold judgment until later

2. "Free-wheeling" is welcome: the wilder the idea the better

3. Quantity is wanted. The more response alternatives a person can generate, the more likely s/he is to arrive at the potentially best ideas for a solution

4. Combination and improvement are sought: two or more ideas may be joined together into a new idea. (p. 114)

It is important in brainstorming alternatives, as in problem identification, to be clear and concrete. Brainstorming as many ideas for solutions to a problem as possible makes it more likely that useful ideas will be identified. Participants should be flexible in their thinking and be encouraged to think of many different options before acting: "In this way they are more likely to have better ideas, less likely to act impulsively, and unlikely to be passive or 'stuck' when faced with a problem or decision" (Elias & Tobias, 1996, p. 7).

Session 7: Evaluating Consequences and Outcomes

Effective problem solving does not stop at brainstorming solutions but includes a process of reviewing and examining potential consequences of using these strategies. Deciding which solution is best involves the use of consequential thinking in evaluating the relative strengths and weaknesses of the available alternatives (Goldstein, 1999). Participants who have been taught to use "if-then" statements in Anger Control Training's "thinking ahead" step can quickly identify with this kind of thinking. They will look at the relevant consequences in terms of long- or short-term outcomes as well as in terms of the social and personal impact on their lives (D'Zurilla et al., 2004).

There are times when youth will choose a solution that fails. The failure of a solution may be the result of the youth's not having learned how to deal with specific situations successfully, or it may be caused by a deficit or interruption in one or more of the problem-solving steps (D'Zurilla & Goldfried, 1971). These failures become a learning experience in which the youth has the opportunity to rethink and become aware of the fact that decision making and problem solving are a process (Elias & Tobias, 1996). The youth may also learn to dialogue with facilitators and peers in the problem-solving process, as well as acquire coping techniques for when a goal must be denied or delayed (Shure, 2001).

Session 8: Problem-Solving Practice—I Can Do It!

Session 8 provides the opportunity to practice the entire problem-solving process. As McGinnis and Goldstein (1997) note:

> Transfer of training has been shown to be enhanced by procedures to maximize over-learning or response availability. . . . That is, the more we have practiced responses (especially *correct* ones), the easier it will be to use them in other contexts or at later times. (p. 208)

In other words, through repetition of the process of finding and implementing solutions to a variety of problems, participants increase their coping skills repertoire. By beginning with less complex problems, youth gain competence and confidence in the process.

IMPLEMENTING PROBLEM-SOLVING TRAINING

Youth encounter problems in all areas of their natural environment and, therefore, the problem-solving process can be taught in a classroom, at a community center, in residential treatment facilities, and especially in the home.

Goldstein's work in teaching prosocial competencies included Skillstreaming and other Prepare Curriculum courses for use with adolescents and younger children alike. The authors have used Problem-Solving Training successfully with children 8 years old and up. It is our belief, and Goldstein's, that problem solving could be the most important of all skills to teach children and youth who must negotiate the struggles of development toward independence. With that understanding, this volume includes problem sample scenarios written for each of the problem-solving concepts. Scenarios for older youth (ages 13–18) appear in the sessions themselves; situations for younger children (ages 8–12) appear in Appendix A.

In teaching problem solving, there is a fine balance between teaching the process and respecting youths' desires to solve their particular problems. Many youth seek a quick fix to their uncomfortable circumstances. Our goal is to slow them down so they can look at different aspects of their situation, be certain they are dealing with only one problem at a time and not a cluster, and develop insight into alternative solutions. When choosing examples of problems to illustrate the step or concept being taught, facilitators should use a fictitious (albeit relevant) situation. Once participants thoroughly understand the process, they may then establish their need to use this process to examine their own specific problems. This teaching method corresponds to the instructional approach in Skillstreaming, where the step-by-step process of performing the skill is more important than the "story." As facilitators and the group observe the practice of problem solving, feedback should focus as much on the steps followed as the solution generated. Additional activities for both age groups to supplement this curriculum are included in Appendix B.

Session Content and Format

As shown in Table 2, training involves instruction in a series of problem-solving steps, taught cumulatively over eight sessions. The training is presented in a series of sequential sessions, taught at a pace that ensures that youth have a good grasp of the concepts before moving on.

The first session provides an overview of Problem-Solving Training. From the second session on, each session follows a standard format:

- Greeting the group (review the rules, lead an icebreaker)
- Review of the previous session's material
- Participant sharing of Problem-Solving Worksheets and description of their problem
- Teaching of the new problem-solving step or concept and optional use of activities to demonstrate practical applications of the steps or concepts (see Appendix B)
- Facilitator modeling of problem-solving step(s)
- Participant practice of problem-solving steps through role-play
- Review of key points in the current lesson

Table 2: Outline of Problem-Solving Training Sessions

Session 1: Overview of Problem Solving

Session 2: Barriers to Problem Solving—Cognitive Distortions/Thinking Errors

Session 3: Problem Signs/Stop and Think

Session 4: Problem Identification

Session 5: Gathering Information (Own and Others' Perspective)

Session 6: Brainstorming Alternatives

Session 7: Evaluating Consequences and Outcomes

Session 8: Problem-Solving Practice: I Can Do It!

- Assignment of interim practice in the form of completion of new Problem-Solving Worksheet

Program Concerns

Group Size and Composition

In line with many of the Prepare Curriculum modules, we recommend a group size of five to eight participants. This number affords a diversity of opinion without jeopardizing the opportunity for all to learn and contribute to the process. Groups may be coeducational or gender specific (depending on the setting and goals of the group) and should be composed of participants in a similar age range.

Facilitators

Facilitators should have the following qualities:

- Comfort working with youth in a group situation
- Good listening and presenting skills
- The ability to lead a group through an entire session by engaging the participants, through the use of humor, interactive techniques, and nonthreatening behavior management
- Knowledge and awareness of Prepare Curriculum components
- Consciousness of cultural issues that may affect the problem-solving process
- Awareness of their own strengths and weaknesses
- Ability to model the problem-solving techniques in their own lives

Setting and Materials

The meeting room should be well lit and have ample space to move about freely when conducting role-plays. Chairs should be set up in a semicircular configuration. Flip charts or another form of whole-group display (whiteboard, chalkboard, PowerPoint) is optimal to allow facilitators to display notes during the session and as a record to return to in future weeks. If whiteboards or chalkboards are used, facilitators should record pertinent information and issues prior to erasing them. Copies of Problem-Solving

Worksheets and other handouts are required. Necessary supplies for the supplementary activities in Appendix B are described there.

Problem-Solving Worksheet. A Problem-Solving Worksheet, tailored for each session, is distributed weekly. Participants are asked to follow the instructions provided and be ready to describe and discuss their experiences at the next Problem-Solving Training meeting.

Problem-Solving Journal. Participants are encouraged to keep their Problem-Solving Worksheets, highlighting their journey as the sessions move along, in a personal Problem-Solving Journal. The journal can be a folder or notebook of any type. Keeping this journal as a record can culminate in participants' gaining insight into how far they have progressed and what useful changes they can make in their real lives.

Parent/Caregiver Involvement

If possible, parents and other caregivers should be given an overview of the problem-solving steps. Potential options could include participation in a Family TIES group (Calame & Parker, 2013), holding an information meeting, sending home a weekly bulletin of the lesson learned or a problem-solving poster to put up in the home, and so forth. Many problems arise in the home setting, and approaching problem solving as a cooperative venture can help youth extend their learning.

Program Evaluation

Fidelity forms are designed to ensure that facilitators accurately follow the recommended steps in program delivery. The Problem-Solving Training Facilitator's Evaluation Form should be completed after each session. This form, and an observer's checklist, are included in Appendix C. Further adherence to implementation integrity can be promoted by videotaping the sessions to be reviewed in peer supervision by a coach, mentor, or master trainer.

Role-Playing

Role-playing is an essential tool for practicing concepts in the problem-solving sequence. Role-playing generally follows the same format as in Skillstreaming, in which the main actor follows the problem-solving steps, the coactor stays in the role of the other person, and the other participants watch for the steps in the role-play that correspond to the problem-solving sequence (Goldstein, 1999).

Each session includes sample situations reflecting typical issues youth may experience. Facilitators may encourage participants to role-play these or use them to model the new problem-solving step or concept. However, whenever possible, the content of modeling displays and role-plays should be derived from participants' real-life situations, as recorded on their Problem-Solving Worksheets.

Enhanced Role-Play Methods

Enhanced role-play methods, prescribed by luke moynahan (2003) in his work with youth on the autism spectrum, are appropriate in Problem-Solving Training. Also used in Social Perception Training (Gundersen, Strømgren, & moynahan, 2013), three techniques are especially useful in helping participants thoroughly appreciate the perspectives they and others have on a problem: the Triple Dance, the Turning Point, and the Four Step.

Triple Dance

The Triple Dance procedure is adapted from the neurolinguistic programming technique developed by Sellæg, Sætrang, and Wroldsen (1993).

To begin:

1. The participant is asked to reconstruct the problematic event by clearly describing what actually happened. Facilitators may need to ask questions in order to get more specific details.

2. The participant watches a role-play of his or her situation performed by others in an attempt to observe and appreciate the dynamics of the problem.

3. Once the participant is satisfied that the situation has been accurately represented in the role-play, he or she then begins to construct the event from the second party's perspective. Facilitators ask questions: How do you think the person felt? What were his or her motives? The participant then role-plays the part of the second party (coactor). In this way, the participant gains an empathic perspective of the problem and then discusses that perspective.

4. The participant then plays the role of main actor in the problem situation, trying now to solve the problem from a more enlightened perspective.

Turning Point

In the Turning Point, a sample scenario or a participant's real problem is presented and acted out by two different actors in a role-play. The participant observes the action without comment or interruption. The role-play is then reenacted, and the observing participant, using an imaginary remote control device, "pauses" the play when he or she notices a time that change could take place (i.e., the turning point). The participant describes what alternative action could take place and "rewinds" the scene. The actors then continue to role-play, or the observing participant may choose to join in at this time to act out the new action.

In this approach, a participant might start the role-play as one character or as an observer and then, when the action stops at a turning point, the facilitator may ask someone else to play the role as the problem solving continues to develop. Role changing may occur several times in the role-play until participants are satisfied with the outcome. If the suggestion(s) lead to a better result, the participant who presented the problem then repeats the role-play, using the improved method as the main actor, further generalizing the learning.

This method allows for all involved to see and appreciate the different perspectives of others and different possible outcomes and to rehearse for a similar problem that may occur in the future.

The Four Step

The Four Step is a variation of the Triple Dance, in which each participant is asked to solve a problem or dispute of some kind. In step 1, the participant observes the problem role-played by others. In step 2, the participant plays the role of coactor; in step 3, he or she plays the role of main actor. Finally, in step 4, the participant has the task of being a "problem mediator." He or she remains neutral and gives advice on both verbal and nonverbal behaviors, which will be helpful to both of the principal parties in resolving the dispute.

Working with Defended Groups

Occasionally, one may encounter a highly defended group, where members are resistant to sharing their problems or feel too vulnerable to do so. In this case, Problem-Solving Worksheets may be handed in the day before the session. The problems are then combined anonymously on a handout and presented to the group. The group then discusses the problems according to the session being taught. The facilitators include the "owner" of the problem in the role-play in the role of main actor, coactor, or another role that accommodates that person's comfort level. The previously described enhanced role-play methods may be helpful with this type of group.

Mutual Help Approach

Borrowing from the EQUIP Program (Gibbs, Potter, & Goldstein, 1995; Potter, Gibbs, & Goldstein, 2001), one can also employ a mutual help format in Problem-Solving Training. This approach involves a peer-helping approach in which meetings are facilitator guided but youth run.

1. After the new problem-solving concept has been taught, the facilitator refers to individual Problem-Solving Worksheets. The meeting is then turned over to the youth. The group decides who needs the most help that day and then awards the meeting to that individual.

2. Group members actively try to understand and solve the problem, using the steps learned in the Problem-Solving Training sessions.

3. The facilitator observes, asks questions, or makes brief comments to get the group to think and to remind them to use the problem-solving procedures.

4. The facilitator provides performance feedback on the group's work and then summarizes the process, highlighting positive points and areas for improvement.

Reinforcement Strategies

To reinforce learning, best practice suggests the use of real problem situations and the setting of meaningful and realistic goals (often reflective of each youth's individual intervention plan). Weekly sharing of participants' experiences at the beginning of each session provides an opportunity for feedback and public recognition of participants' efforts. Verbal support and encouragement of this kind are among potent reinforcers that can lead to lasting change.

If a system to provide them is in place, tokens or other rewards may be provided to reinforce participants' efforts. Rewards may be provided at the end of each session; however, there is also merit in delaying reinforcement. An example of this would involve the group's trying to complete a puzzle to reach an end of program goal: The group decides on an outing in which they would all like to participate. They draw a poster of the event, cut it into pieces, and mount a poster frame on a wall. Group members receive a piece of the puzzle when they demonstrate sound problem-solving techniques, then place the piece in the appropriate spot within the frame. Once the puzzle has been assembled, the group goes on the outing. To take this exercise a step further, facilitators may encourage the group to look at and define the obstacles in reaching the goal (e.g., session participation and effort, being able to pay for the outing, choosing the right time) and to consider the specific changes that need to be made to attain it.

Incorporating Skillstreaming and Supplementary Activities

In keeping with the multimodal approach of the Prepare Curriculum, the teaching of social skills can complement Problem-Solving Training sessions. As recommended by D'Zurilla and Nezu (1999), one must teach not only the process of finding solutions but also the steps to carrying out those solutions. By teaching youth social skills, we provide them with a concept and a language that enhances the problem-solving process. Table 3 includes some suggestions from the Prepare Curriculum's Skillstreaming course. Skillstreaming posters for these and other skills, available from the publisher of this book, are an excellent aid to the techniques of Problem-Solving Training sessions.

Confucius says, "Tell me, and I will forget. Show me, and I will remember. Involve me, and I will understand." Goldstein (1999) states that many youth lacking in interpersonal skills may be described accurately as action-oriented and relatively nonverbal. Hands-on experiences are therefore particularly effective in challenging them to solve problems as a group. As noted previously, Appendix B includes a number of exercises and ideas that can supplement basic Problem-Solving Training procedures. Appendix D provides a brief description of the Back-up Aggression Replacement Training (BART) program, which employs problem-solving and skills training methods to help youth overcome a behavioral crisis and return to their regular placement living environment.

Table 3: Social Skills to Augment Problem-Solving Training

Session Topic	Suggested Skill
1. Problem-Solving Overview	Arranging Problems by Importance (Skill 48)
2. Thinking Errors	Responding to Failure (Skill 38)
3. Problem Signs/Stop and Think	Using Self-Control (Skill 26)
4. Problem Identification	Deciding What Caused a Problem (Skill 44)
5. Gathering Information	
Own Perspective	Deciding on Your Abilities (Skill 46)
Others' Perspective	Gathering Information (Skill 47)
6. Brainstorming Alternatives	Setting a Goal (Skill 45)
7. Evaluating Consequences and Outcomes	Making a Decision (Skill 49)

PART 2

Problem-Solving Training Sessions

SESSION 1
Overview of Problem Solving

RATIONALE

In this session, an overview of the program is delivered and a commitment to participate is elicited from the youth. In real life, problem solving does not always occur according to the neatly ordered steps laid out here and in the Prepare Curriculum. These steps may change in their order, may interact with each other, and/or overlap. According to D'Zurilla and Goldfried (1971), central to the problem-solving approach is the goal not simply to describe the actual problem-solving process, but rather to present a way to help youth organize and use these problem-solving procedures to meet their own needs. An individual's general orientation can greatly influence the way in which he or she responds to a situation. This orientation will likely influence independent problem-solving needs that will require: (a) accepting that problematic situations are a normal part of life and that coping with most of these situations effectively is possible, (b) recognizing problematic situations when they occur, and (c) avoiding the tendency to respond impulsively or to do nothing.

MATERIALS

Steps in Problem Solving handout

Steps in Problem Solving poster (created before the session begins)

Problem-Solving Journals (folders or notebooks, one per participant)

Flip chart or whiteboard

SESSION PLAN

Introduction

Begin the session with an icebreaker activity to facilitate group formation, building a relationship between the facilitators and participants. The Birthday Lineup is both a problem-solving activity and one where all may share a bit about themselves.

The Birthday Lineup

1. Explain to the group there are many ways to communicate with people other than by using your voice. Everyone, including facilitators, lines up in order, with January 1 birthdays at one end of the line and December 31 birthdays at the other end of the line. There is only one rule: No one may speak.

2. When the line is finished being formed, ask everyone in the line to say his or her name, birth date, and favorite snack food. (This information may provide ideas for facilitators who wish to bring snacks to the sessions.)

Expectations and Procedures

Have the group members take their seats and continue the session by explaining expectations and procedures:

- Inform the youth of the dates and times of the sessions.

- Ask the youth to come up with their own set of rules, thereby instilling in them a sense of ownership of the group. If they seem incapable, hesitant, or resistant, direct them by asking leading questions—for example, "What if someone talks about what you say in the group outside the group itself? What would be a rule the group could agree upon that addresses the issue?" Then have the group write a rule of their own design about confidentiality. It could be "What is said in the group stays in the group." Encourage similar rules concerning respect for others' opinions, use of appropriate language, need for everyone's active participation in the group, and so forth. Rules should be positively expressed. In other words, "Use appropriate language" is more appropriate than "No swearing." Record the name of the person(s) who suggested the rule and in the future refer to it as "Timothy's rule" or "Ruth's rule." Enforcing the rules can be more easily achieved when it has been the group members who have actually been responsible for their creation.

- Write down the rules on a flip chart or whiteboard and later create a poster (or have group members create a poster) to display the rules during all following sessions. Facilitators and youth can then hold one another accountable to the rules they themselves created.

Introduction to Problem Solving

1. Introduce the session by asking the following questions:

   What is a problem?

   Generate answers from the group. Make the following points in the discussion:

   - We make decisions every day (e.g., getting up or deciding what to eat). Many of these decisions are not problematic.

   - Decisions are harder to make when they involve more complicated problem situations.

   - A problem is a situation one faces where there is an obstacle or obstacles that prevent us from reaching a goal or experiencing the desired outcome.

   Explain that problems are difficult situations that we are not exactly sure what to do about. They can be simple (e.g., You can't find your favorite shirt) or more complicated (e.g., You promised to visit your grandmother, and you receive a call from your friend inviting you to a party on the same night.)

Why solve problems?

Generate answers from the group. Discuss the following:

- What are the benefits? (To achieve your goals in spite of obstacles, feel less stress, etc.)

- What happens when you ignore problems or don't try to solve them? (Problems can become worse or more complicated to solve. However, one must carefully consider if problems are better left alone or will likely resolve themselves in a reasonable time frame.)

Ask the group for examples of situations when they (a) solved a problem and (b) ignored a problem. What was the outcome in each case?

2. Point out that problems can more often be solved when approached systematically. Explain:

> This program examines the dynamics and steps of problem solving and teaches a process to be used to achieve success. A person doesn't have to do the first thing that comes to mind or give up and do nothing. (Examples: fighting to solve a problem or letting others make your decisions for you.) By learning how to approach problem solving more slowly and carefully, we have more control over what happens to us and may avoid making matters worse. For instance, by thinking about how friends think or feel, we can say and do things that will make it more likely that we'll get along well.

Steps in Problem Solving

Provide copies of the Steps in Problem Solving handout, then discuss the following information. (Participants may follow along on the handout or poster.)

Step 1: Problem Signs

> The first step in successful problem solving is to learn to recognize that you are experiencing one or more problems.

Step 2: Stop and Think

> Stop and Think means taking the time or a step back from a situation to look at and think about the different parts of the problem. Remember to consider if the situation is composed of a number of problems that need to be dealt with, one at a time.

Step 3: Problem Identification (Goals + Obstacles = Problem)

> It is important to be able to define your problem and understand exactly what it is. Every problem has two elements: a goal and an obstacle. If you don't have both, you don't have a problem. Problem solving requires that you state what you want (a goal) in as detailed and precise a way as possible. Once you establish your goal, you need to determine what is stopping you from getting what you want (the obstacles).

In order to "own the problem," special emphasis must be on obstacles you have control of, can have an impact on, or have created yourself.

Problem solvers consider a third element along with goal and obstacles. This third element is change. In other words, you decide what change(s) are needed to get past the obstacle and reach the goal.

Step 4: Gathering Information

This is where we separate the facts from opinions, knowledge versus guessing or rumors. To do a good job of identifying the obstacles and establishing the goals, gathering information is important. In problem solving, we need to take into account information from our own perspective as well as from the point of view of others.

Step 5: Brainstorming Alternatives

There is always more than one approach to solving any problem. The first solution that comes to mind is not always the best. It is essential to think of many different ways to solve the problem. If there is time, bouncing your choices off people you trust and getting their suggestions may be helpful. This is another way to Gather Information from Others' Perspective.

Step 6: Evaluating Consequences and Outcomes

This is an important learning step. One of the most effective ways to look at predicting an outcome for a given problem is to list all outcomes first, look at their potential consequences, arrange them from best to worst, choose one outcome, and try it.

After the fact, by studying the outcome of your solution you can decide if, faced with the problem again, you would make the same changes. Perhaps if things did not work out the way you wanted, you can consider what you might do instead the next time.

Review

1. Briefly review the main points of the session.
2. Give each participant a Problem-Solving Journal. Have group members put their "Steps in Problem Solving" handout in their journal. Explain that they will add more materials to their journals as the sessions progress.

NOTE

It is important to note that the equation presented in this session (*Goal + Obstacles = Problem*) reflects the amount of control the problem solver perceives in using problem-solving techniques. Once a goal is understood as one's own, then the obstacle must be identified. It is important to recognize that one can easily externalize the problem (e.g., "It was his fault—he made me do it!" or "That person cut me off!"), thereby diminishing the perceived amount of direct control one has over the solution. This can create complications as one wastes energy trying to change things beyond one's control. It is better to teach the youth to spend their energy on what they *can* do. Youth frequently identify obstacles that are, in fact, thinking errors. This type of thinking will be discussed in Session 2.

Step 1: Problem Signs

Step 2: Stop and Think

Step 3: Problem Identification

Step 4: Gathering Information

Step 5: Brainstorming Alternatives

Step 6: Evaluating Consequences and Outcomes

Remember to check for Thinking Errors at each step!

SESSION 2

Barriers to Problem Solving: Cognitive Distortions/Thinking Errors

RATIONALE

Often, those who have problem-solving deficits engage in cognitive distortions such as self-centeredness, blaming others, and assuming the worst to justify their behaviors. This session integrates the notion of cognitive distortions (Thinking Errors) and their effects on prosocial problem solving. To recognize that a thinking error exists, it must be pointed out to the person that his or her thought process is inaccurate and, if continued, can be self-destructive or compromise control of the situation. Thinking errors are present everywhere in life. We regard them as "errors" solely from the perspective of responsibility and from the standpoint of society. As we attempt to understand thinking errors, we might be worried to find that, to a degree, we all have some of the characteristics of distorted thinking. To bring about change, however, we must counteract our conviction that we do not need to improve and challenge distorted thinking.

MATERIALS

Thinking Errors handout

Problem-Solving Worksheet 1

Flip chart or whiteboard

SESSION PLAN

Introduction and Review

1. Review the group rules and lead an icebreaker.
2. Review Session 1. Point out that problems are part of life and that with practice you can learn to make decisions about them rather than acting too quickly or letting someone else decide for you.

Thinking Errors

1. Explain to the youth that sometimes people see problems differently. They may be thinking incorrectly about a situation and may inadvertently be contributing to making the problem worse or harder to solve. Describe the following Thinking Errors as typical ways people do this. Provide an example of each that is relevant to the group.

   Self-Centered

   Thinking that your own needs and feelings are the only ones or are more important than those of others. To find a solution to a problem, you must also take into consideration the needs and perspective of all others involved.

   Assuming the Worst

   Assuming that, no matter what, things aren't going to work out well, no matter how hard you try. When you believe others are thinking poorly of you, you are thinking negatively of others. When you have no confidence in your own ability, you are assuming there is no solution.

   Expecting Hostility

   This is similar to *Assuming the Worst* but also includes interpreting ambiguous behaviors by others as deliberately hostile acts. It may be a result of remembering hurtful events of the past. As well, one's negative self-talk and feelings may trigger incorrect interpretations that someone is a threat to his or her well-being or the well-being of others.

   Blaming Others

   Not taking responsibility for your own thoughts and actions and blaming others for your harmful behavior when it's really your fault or blaming innocent others for your misfortunes or victimization. Therefore, a problem solver's focus should be on what he or she can knows or can own about the situation. We can work only on what we know to be true and change that which is our own.

   Minimizing

   Thinking that your problems or behaviors aren't as bad as they really are or that they won't cause any harm to yourself or others. When you undervalue your part in the problem situation, you reduce the impact you can have on solving it.

2. Distribute copies of the Thinking Errors handout. Have the group complete it, then discuss. Ask the group for some examples of their own. (Answers: 1-S, 2-B, 3-A, 4-E, 5-M, 6-B, 7-M, 8-B, 9-A, 10-S, 11-A, 12-E)

Problem-Solving Worksheet

1. Provide copies of Problem-Solving Worksheet 1. In this worksheet, group members are asked to give their feedback on the scenario provided and to record a situation during the week in which they have or have not used problem solving.

2. Explain the importance of the Problem-Solving Worksheets:

- They give an accurate report, on a weekly basis, of problems or challenging issues group members have faced.
- They help group members figure out what their problem situations are and begin thinking about how they can handle problems effectively.
- They provide material for the role-play of problem-solving techniques.

3. Discuss the example shown on the Problem-Solving Worksheet, including the nature of the problem and any Thinking Errors that may be present.

Review and Practice

1. Briefly review the main points of the session and answer any questions.
2. Have participants put their Thinking Errors handout and Problem-Solving Worksheet in their journals.
3. Let the group know that their practice before the next session is to complete the Problem-Solving Worksheet by identifying a problem and any associated Thinking Errors. Let the group know that they will have the opportunity to discuss their worksheets at the beginning of the next session.

NOTE

You may wish to supplement the session with the *EQUIPPED for Life Game* (Horn, Shively, & Gibbs, 2007), available from Research Press at the address given on this book's title page.

Thinking Errors

Name _____ Date _____

Identify the following statements as Self-Centered (S), Assuming the Worst (A), Blaming Others (B), Minimizing (M), or Expecting Hostility (E).

_____ 1. I'm cold. I'm just going to take this coat on the coat rack.

_____ 2. What fool left $20 on the table? It's mine now!

_____ 3. There's no point in studying for the test. I'm going to fail anyway.

_____ 4. "What are you looking at? You got a problem with me?"

_____ 5. I broke her cell phone. Her parents are rich; they'll just buy her a new one.

_____ 6. The kid looked so stupid, I ripped him off.

_____ 7. I pushed him, but he isn't really that hurt. No big deal.

_____ 8. It's my social worker's fault I'm here. She wrote a bad report.

_____ 9. I'm late, so why go home now? I'll be grounded anyway.

_____ 10. I steal DVDs because I've got to have something to watch, don't I?

_____ 11. He's going to fire me because I just broke up with his daughter.

_____ 12. I'm pregnant. My dad's going to lay a beating on me.

From *Problem-Solving Training,* by K. Parker, R. Calame, K. K. Gundersen, A. Simon, J. Choi, & M. Amendola, © 2013, Champaign, IL: Research Press (800-519-2707, www.researchpress.com).

Problem-Solving Worksheet 1: Problems and Thinking Errors

Name _____ Date _____

Read the following problem situation.

You have promised your father that you will clean the storage area together with him this afternoon. On the way home from school you start talking with your friends and only arrive home for supper. You are surprised when you arrive home and your father is upset with you.

What is the problem?

_____

_____

_____

_____

Circle the **Thinking Error(s):**

    Self-Centered

    Minimizing

    Blaming Others

    Assuming the Worst

    Expecting Hostility

Describe a problem you have had lately.

_____

_____

_____

_____

Circle the **Thinking Error(s):**

    Self-Centered

    Minimizing

    Blaming Others

    Assuming the Worst

    Expecting Hostility

From *Problem-Solving Training,* by K. Parker, R. Calame, K. K. Gundersen, A. Simon, J. Choi, & M. Amendola, © 2013, Champaign, IL: Research Press (800-519-2707, www.researchpress.com).

SESSION 3
Problem Signs/Stop and Think

RATIONALE

This is the time for participants to realize that problems are normal and that they must reflect on doing something that is not impulsive and that taps into their own problem-solving abilities. In our experience, it has always been valuable to have the group recognize that the first symptom of a problem is usually a change in mood or feelings. Having people become sensitive to these clues or cues can help them realize it is time to stop and think.

MATERIALS

Magazine pictures showing interactions among several people

Flip chart or whiteboard

Problem-Solving Worksheet 2

SESSION PLAN

Introduction and Review

1. Review the group rules and lead an icebreaker.
2. Review Thinking Errors. Have participants go over Problem-Solving Worksheet 1 and discuss their problem and potential Thinking Errors. Provide reinforcement for successful use and, at the same time, check the worksheets to see that they are filled in correctly.

Problem Signs

1. Explain:

> Problems are a part of everybody's life and everyone can be better at solving them. The first step in successful problem solving is to learn how to recognize problems. To know that you are experiencing a problem, you must first observe exactly what is happening and recognize how you feel and think. Our emotional and physical responses to problem situations often happen when we first encounter a problem.

2. Discuss with the group that to be a good problem solver you have to be a good detective and notice all the clues that there is a problem, regardless of their intensity. Explain that these clues are sometimes called "cues."

- *Physical Cues:* What is going on in your body (upset stomach, tension, nervousness, trembling, trouble sleeping, etc.)?
- *Emotional Cues:* What is happening on an emotional level to you or those who are with you? Has the mood changed? Are there feelings of hurt, anger, disappointment, confusion, etc.?

You can use the following real-life scenario to illustrate the importance of recognizing problem signs:

> When a fire alarm goes off, your physical cues may be that your heart races, you tense up, or you feel a need to move quickly. Your emotional cues may be that you are worried, scared, confused, or alert. Most of us learn by trial and error and natural consequences that fire can burn and cause pain. Through this experience, people learn to avoid fire. Our choices are determined by how quickly we couple the danger signs with our personal experience. When the alarm rings in a fire drill, people quickly recognize the problem and follow the protocol of orderly and safe evacuation of the building. A firefighter, using a different problem-solving skill set, will go into the danger in a trained and prepared fashion to put out the fire, save people, etc.

3. Using magazine pictures that show detailed interactions among several people, ask the group members to explain what they see, in terms of physical and emotional cues, and what they think the problem might be. Point out that not everyone sees the same thing. Define the problem in the picture differently by using different details from two group members to show how different observations affect the definition of the problem.

4. Explain that people can have a lot of different reactions to problems and that you need to learn to recognize that you have a problem by how you think and feel. Instruct participants to do the following:

- *Examine different thoughts:* Most of the time you just won't know what to do. You'll have questions and doubts, and not be sure what is best. You may know what you want, but you can't figure out how to get it.
- *Examine different feelings:* Many times you'll have uncomfortable feelings that let you know you have a problem. You may feel frustrated, tense, restless, or confused about your choices.

5. Ask group members to describe their own reactions to problems and write them down on the flip chart or whiteboard. Compare their list to the common reactions shown in Table 4. Add any they have not suggested.

6. Ask participants to discuss the physical and emotional cues they experienced in the problems they identified in Problem-Solving Worksheet 1.

Table 4: Stop and Think—Common Reactions to Problems

Discouraged	Uncertain	Put down
Feel like giving up	Annoyed	Questioning
Restless	Frustrated	Sleepy
Worried	Unhappy	Feel like you can't make the best decision anyway
Want to escape	Sad	Want to do anything just to get it done
Inadequate	Tense	
Confused	Uncomfortable	Want to avoid by doing something else
Angry	Doubtful	

From *The Prepare Curriculum: Teaching Prosocial Competencies* (p. 523), © 1999 by A.P. Goldstein, Champaign, IL: Research Press. Reprinted by permission.

Stop and Think

Refocus

1. State that successful problem solving depends on thinking before you act. Explain that if we ignore our cues and fail to take the time to stop and think, we may make hasty decisions and poor choices. We need to take the time to think of different ways to solve the problem and choose the best one. Encourage participants to start to pay attention to, and become more familiar with, their physical and emotional cues as they encounter a problem.

2. Explain that taking a few deep breaths and saying to yourself "Stop and Think" will give you time to decide what you want to do. Point out that proper breathing is a powerful tool in helping to regain our focus in using Stop and Think. Compare the gentle breathing of a sleeping baby to the labored breathing of a stressed adult to demonstrate the differences. The calm breath of a baby, where the stomach and chest slowly fills, is more relaxed than the shallow and rapid breath from the adult's chest. Have the youth put their hands on their abdomens and practice breathing deeply. Have them try some shallow chest breathing. Ask them which way calms them more effectively. When they are calm, do they think it is easier to think more clearly?

Point out that competitive athletes are aware of how proper breathing can enhance their performance. Singers, dancers, and other performers also use breathing techniques to maximize their abilities. In addition, many forms of meditation and relaxation techniques (e.g., yoga, Tai Chi, Conscious Connected Breathing, etc.) emphasize how breathing helps focus and soothe the body: mentally, physically, and spiritually.

Use a Reminder

Inform participants that saying "Stop and Think" to yourself can be a reminder. It is a good example of self-directive and positive self-talk.

Role-Playing

1. Model a problem situation (with your co-facilitator, if necessary). Use a situation relevant to the group or, if need be, one of the following examples. Ask and answer the following questions:

   - What is the problem?
   - What are the Problem Signs?
   - When should I take a deep breath and Stop and Think?
   - What are the Thinking Error(s)?

   ### Situation 1

   You and your friends are arguing about where to go out for supper. You always want to go for pizza. Your friends accuse you of always being selfish and thinking about yourself first.

   ### Situation 2

   Your brand new running shoes are missing. Charlie said he wanted a pair just like yours. You say to yourself, "I'll bet Charlie stole them."

2. Have participants role-play situations from their Problem-Solving Worksheets:

   Problem Signs + Stop and Think + Thinking Errors

   When coaching/observing main actors, make sure that they can identify the signs that they have a problem. They also must take a deep breath and remind themselves to Stop and Think.

3. Conduct performance feedback: As in Skillstreaming, feedback should be based on how the main actor performed the problem-solving steps, not just on the solution chosen.

   - *Coactor:* Not all role-plays will involve a coactor. However, if there is one, ask the coactor to give feedback to the main actor on how he or she performed the problem-solving steps.
   - *Observers:* Ask all the observers how they thought the main actor performed the problem-solving steps learned to date. For example:

   Observer 1: Jane, I heard you identify your problem signs. You said that your stomach did a flip-flop and you were feeling anxious.

   Observer 2: Jane, I saw you take a deep breath, Stop and Think, and say, "Uh-oh! I think this is a problem."

   Observer 3: Jane, I think you were jumping to conclusions, and you didn't ask yourself if there was a Thinking Error. I think you may have been Assuming the Worst. What do you think?

   - *Facilitator(s):* Next the facilitator(s) gives feedback, using the following steps:
     a. Look at the person you are evaluating.

b. Identify the positive use of the problem-solving steps used in the role-play to quickly reinforce the main actor's positive performance.

c. Use "I-statements" when you give feedback. Say, "I think you did this or that aspect skillfully" and explain what you saw.

d. When you observe something weak about the role-play, also use an I-statement. It is always good practice to give the actor something to "grow on." Rather than say, "You did this poorly, and you should try such and such," try to say something like "If I were you, I would have said or done such and such." This strategy causes the recipient of the feedback to feel helped or encouraged rather than criticized.

- *Main actor:* Finally, ask the main actor how he or she feels about the role-play.

Review and Practice

1. Briefly review the main points of the session and answer any questions.

2. Hand out the new Problem-Solving Worksheet and ask group members to complete it before the next session.

NOTE

The process of identifying problem signs and using Stop and Think clarifies and binds the problem to the individual. If the youth is indifferent to the problem or has a "couldn't care less" attitude, there is neither ownership nor motivation to find a solution. That is to say, if you don't own it, you can't change it!

Problem-Solving Worksheet 2: Problem Signs/Stop and Think

Name _____ Date _____

Read the following problem situation.

You were at the hairdresser last night. She cut your hair shorter than you wanted. You walk into the class and everyone laughs. Your face gets hot, and you are embarrassed.

What is the problem?

_____

_____

What are your **Problem Signs?**

Physical: _____

Emotional: _____

When should you take a deep breath and **Stop and Think?** _____

Circle the **Thinking Error(s):**

    Self-Centered

    Minimizing

    Blaming Others

    Assuming the Worst

    Expecting Hostility

Describe a problem you have or have had lately.

What is the problem?

_____

_____

What are your **Problem Signs?**

Physical: _____

Emotional: _____

When should you take a deep breath and **Stop and Think?** _____

Circle the **Thinking Error(s):**

    Self-Centered

    Minimizing

    Blaming Others

    Assuming the Worst

    Expecting Hostility

From *Problem-Solving Training,* by K. Parker, R. Calame, K. K. Gundersen, A. Simon, J. Choi, & M. Amendola, © 2013, Champaign, IL: Research Press (800-519-2707, www.researchpress.com).

SESSION 4
Problem Identification

RATIONALE

When an individual recognizes a problem situation and avoids making an automatic response, he or she then needs to proceed to using the elements of problem identification. These are (a) defining the problem and (b) classifying elements of the situation by separating irrelevant information, primary goals, and major obstacles. For an effective process to occur, the problem solver must be clear and specific when identifying the problem, the goal, and the obstacles.

MATERIALS

Problem-Solving Worksheet 3

Flip chart or whiteboard

SESSION PLAN

Introduction and Review

1. Review the group rules and lead an icebreaker.

2. Referring to the Problem-Solving poster or worksheet, review the steps learned to date, using an example relevant to participants and model each step using self-talk (i.e., being aware of physical and emotional cues and the importance of Stop and Think).

3. Have group members discuss their use of Problem-Solving Worksheet 2. For their own personal scenarios, have them describe their problem and identify their Problem Signs, use of Stop and Think, and potential Thinking Errors. Provide reinforcement for successful use and check the worksheets to see that they are filled in correctly.

Defining a Problem

1. Explain that problem solving is a plan that helps us to work on most problems. It helps to break down a problem into manageable parts that you can organize easily. If you have difficulty solving problems, it is often because you are unsure of exactly what the problem is or are too focused on the related feelings. The most important part of this step is learning to say what the problem is as clearly and as specifically as you can.

2. Explain that you can't solve a problem that is too complex or unclear or too broadly or narrowly defined.

   - Give an example of a problem that has been too broadly defined. For example, you can say that getting along with teachers is your problem, but this really tells very little about what it is that teachers do that bothers you.

   - Give an example of a problem too narrowly defined. For example, you can say that your problem is Mr. Jones's yelling, but this gives too little information about the type of problem as a whole: The problem can be why Mr. Jones is yelling or how it is affecting you.

3. Explain that there may be times when you discover that you are trying to solve more than one problem at a time. In that case, you must determine which problem should be worked on first. For example, you want to go to trade school to learn to be a mechanic in spite of your parents wanting you to go to college. You don't have the grades for either and want to keep up your busy social life.

4. Explain that, in order to make good decisions, you have to ask yourself questions to get at exactly what the problem is. If you're having a bad feeling, you've got a problem! Discuss the following questions you can ask yourself:

What is my goal?

Often people get sidetracked by an obstacle and lose sight of their goal. Remind participants to use "I-statements" that ensure that they are owning the problem or ask themselves the question "What do I really want?"

What don't I like?

Have participants think about their problem signs and how the situation made them feel. Have them ask themselves why there was a shift in their emotions. Was it because they were feeling offended, scared, challenged, or something else? (When participants discuss "What don't I like?" it is important to have them avoid blaming external forces and focus instead on owning their part in the problem.)

What are my obstacle(s)?

Have participants visualize a concrete situation. For example, you are on your way to an appointment. Your goal is to get to your appointment on time. You encounter your first obstacle when you discover that your car is running and the keys are locked inside. This obstacle can seem simple but, more often than not, people get lost in thoughts like "I'm late! Stupid car! The engine is running! What are the people waiting for me going to say?" and experience feelings of frustration, anger, and disbelief. The real obstacle at this point becomes panicking or worrying about things that can't be changed at the moment. These Thinking Errors (specifically, Assuming the Worst) only create more problems. It is important first to identify and correct these errors. In the moment, it may be more helpful to think, "I'm getting too angry too quickly."

What do I need to change?

Point out that once you have looked more specifically at the goal and obstacles, relevant solutions begin to become more apparent.

5. Remind the group that *Goals + Obstacles = Problem*. Apply the questions they can ask themselves to the situation previously described:

- What is my goal? (I need to get to my appointment.)
- What don't I like? (I'm going to be late.)
- What are my obstacle(s)? (I am panicking and the keys are locked in the car.)
- What do I need to change? (I need to Stop and Think. I need to make a call to get help to open my car door or find another way to get to the appointment.)

Role-Playing

1. Model a problem situation (with your co-facilitator, if necessary). Use a situation relevant to the group or, if need be, one of the following examples. Ask and answer the following questions:

- What is the problem?
- What are the Problem Signs?
- When should I take a deep breath and Stop and Think?
- What are the Thinking Error(s)?
- What is my goal?
- What are the obstacle(s)?
- What change do I need to make?

Situation 1

You are working hard on a history project at school and you think it is pretty good. You still have a lot to do but it is due to be handed in to the teacher in 30 minutes.

Situation 2

You are looking for a job and pass by a local grocery store. A sign in the window says "Help Wanted: Weekends and Evenings." You are available to work on weekends, but they probably won't hire you because you have to study during the week.

2. Ask each group member to give an example of a problem from his or her Problem-Solving Worksheet, identifying both the goals and obstacles. Using one or more of these examples, have group members role-play:

Problem Signs + Stop and Think + Thinking Errors + Problem Identification

3. Conduct performance feedback in the prescribed order: coactor, observers, facilitator(s), and main actor.

Review and Practice

1. Review the main points of the session.
2. Hand out the new Problem-Solving Worksheet and ask group members to complete it before the next session.

NOTE

Participants may have the tendency to mix up their goals with obstacles and therefore get sidetracked. The facilitator must keep the group focused on the problem by coaching them to respond specifically to the problem at hand. When the steps are recorded, it may become apparent that there is a better goal. Writing things out can often lead to clarification, recognition, and reorganization of the goals, obstacles, and changes needed.

Problem-Solving Worksheet 3: Problem Identification

Name _____ Date _____

Read the following problem situation.

Your younger sister is always coming in your room and bugging you. One day you give her a shove out of your room. She isn't really hurt, but you are grounded. You feel that she set you up and the punishment is unfair.

What is the problem?

_____

_____

What are your **Problem Signs?**

Physical: _____

Emotional: _____

When should you take a deep breath and **Stop and Think?** _____

Circle the **Thinking Error(s):**

> Self-Centered
>
> Minimizing
>
> Blaming Others
>
> Assuming the Worst
>
> Expecting Hostility

Problem Identification

What is my goal? _____

What is it I don't like? _____

What are the obstacle(s)? _____

What change do I need to make? _____

From *Problem-Solving Training,* by K. Parker, R. Calame, K. K. Gundersen, A. Simon, J. Choi, & M. Amendola, © 2013, Champaign, IL: Research Press (800-519-2707, www.researchpress.com).

Describe a problem you have or have had lately.

What is the problem?

_____

_____

What are your **Problem Signs?**

Physical: _____

Emotional: _____

When should you take a deep breath and **Stop and Think?** _____

Circle the **Thinking Error(s):**

    Self-Centered

    Minimizing

    Blaming Others

    Assuming the Worst

    Expecting Hostility

Problem Identification

What is my goal? _____

What is it I don't like? _____

What are the obstacle(s)? _____

What change do I need to make? _____

SESSION 5

Gathering Information (Own and Others' Perspective)

RATIONALE

To avoid making impulsive or misinformed decisions, it is necessary to carefully examine all facets of the problem. This holds true not only when the problem is new or unfamiliar, but also when it frequently reoccurs. Good decisions are based on gathering and considering as many perspectives on the matter as possible. When gathering perspectives, it is important for participants to learn to separate fact from opinion. This may involve differentiating between reality and egocentric bias, challenging pessimistic views of others or oneself, avoiding assumptions, and accepting responsibility.

MATERIALS

Fact Versus Opinion Handout

Problem-Solving Worksheet 4

Flip chart or whiteboard

SESSION PLAN

Review

1. Review the group rules and lead an icebreaker.

2. Have participants discuss the scenario provided on their Problem-Solving Worksheets. Then have them describe their problem and identify their Problem Signs. Then proceed with Stop and Think, Thinking Errors, and Problem Identification, as applied to their own personal situations.

3. Referring to the Problem-Solving poster or worksheet, review the steps learned to date, using an example relevant to participants and model each step using self-talk.

Gathering Information (Own Perspective)

1. Ask group members how many times they have reacted to a situation where only a little information was available. As more information came to light, have they regretted their reaction or had to change their response? Explain that sometimes the problem actually changes once you have gotten all the information you can. You

need to gather this information by "being a detective" and gathering clues and by using the tools all your senses provide.

2. Suggest that it is easy to confuse what we think a problem is with what it really is. One reason is that we confuse facts and opinions.

   - *Ask:* What is a fact? Write down as many responses as you can solicit from the group. Point out that a fact is what we have evidence for, something we are sure of.

   - *Ask:* What is an opinion? Obtain some responses and write them down. Point out that an opinion is what we think is happening, something we feel or assume. Explain that different people often have different ideas on what they think is happening—in other words, they have different opinions. However, different people would likely agree on the facts—what they actually know is happening. Ask the group which category rumors fall into.

3. Distribute copies of the Fact Versus Opinion handout. Have the group use it to practice distinguishing fact from opinion. (Answers: 1-O, 2-O, 3-F, 4-F, 5-O, 6-O, 7-F, 8-O, 9-O, 10-F)

Gathering Information (Others' Perspective)

1. Emphasize that most problems in some way involve other people. What is really going on involves not only oneself but also what the other person is experiencing. It is important, therefore, to get as much information as possible on the perspective of the other people involved in the problem or situation to gain an accurate understanding. It is useful to know as much as possible about what the other people think, feel, and believe.

2. Ask the group how they can know what a person is thinking, feeling, and believing. Stress that, when gathering information, it is important to consider all five senses: sight, hearing, touch, smell, and taste. Be sure to discuss body language, facial expression, tone of voice, spoken and written words, and so forth. For example: A woman is yelling frantically at you to get out of the way as you are walking up a busy staircase. You don't know this person and you think this woman is rude. In fact, her child has fallen sick and has just been taken to the hospital. She is rushing to get to her child and really was not even aware of you. In this situation, you can look for the nonverbal clues as to the other person's perspective.

   - Are you looking at an angry face or a worried one? Can you determine what is fact or opinion?

   - Is the woman looking at you or past you (to where she needs to get to)?

   - Is the woman's tone of voice threatening or more an expression of urgency?

3. Point out that another way to gather information from another's perspective is to ask direct questions of the person involved, assuming it is an appropriate time and place.

Role-Playing

1. Model a problem situation (with your co-facilitator, if necessary). Use a situation relevant to the group or, if need be, one of the following examples. Ask and answer the following questions:

   - What is the problem?
   - What are the Problem Signs?
   - When should I take a deep breath and Stop and Think?
   - What are the Thinking Error(s)?
   - What is my goal?
   - What are the obstacle(s)?
   - What change do I need to make?
   - What information can I gather from myself? From others?

Situation 1

You are gay and want to go to the school dance. You are tired of hiding your relationship and demand that your partner comes with you. Your partner says, "No, I'm not ready for that."

Situation 2

You want to buy a new MP3 player but don't have enough money to afford a major brand name. You go into the store and find a new one you can afford that has a warranty. Beside it, for the same price, is the number-one brand in an open box but with no warranty.

Situation 3

Your good friend comes up to you at lunch hour and tells you that there is a guy who has been trying to take his girlfriend away from him. He is very angry and wants your help to confront the guy after school. It will probably end up in a fight.

2. Using examples from their Problem-Solving Worksheets, have participants role-play:

   Problem Signs + Stop and Think + Problem Identification + Thinking Errors + Gathering Information (Own and Others' Perspective)

3. Conduct performance feedback in the prescribed order: coactor, observers, facilitator(s), and main actor.

Review and Practice

1. Briefly review the main points of the session and answer any questions.

2. Hand out the new Problem-Solving Worksheet to be added to participants' personal journals. (From this session onward, the Problem-Solving Worksheets focus solely on participants' problem situations.)

NOTE

Although the Prepare Curriculum breaks this session into two lessons, in our experience, these concepts can be taught in one session. There should, however, be no rush to complete the training and one must tailor the pace to the clientele. An additional session could be added at this point, if required.

A lot of fun is possible with this session. You can use tools or examples where one can practice discerning between fact and opinion—news stories versus fictional accounts, for example. You can also provide optical illusions, tongue twisters, misleading logic games, science experiments, activities that test balance or judgment, and the like. Use themes or activities that challenge all five senses. Examples of these types of activities can be found in Appendix B.

Fact Versus Opinion

Identify the following as fact (F) or opinion (O).

_____ 1. She is 18 years old! Of course she has her driver's license!

_____ 2. Judging by how tall he is, he is a good basketball player.

_____ 3. Insurance rates are higher for new young drivers.

_____ 4. The picnic has been canceled due to rain.

_____ 5. Jon's door just slammed. He must be really mad.

_____ 6. It's all right to jaywalk because the police never fine you for that.

_____ 7. The doctor told me to ice my ankle after spraining it.

_____ 8. It's Thursday night. There's no way I'll have homework!

_____ 9. I think Jennifer is going to quit school.

_____ 10. If our team does not win this final game, we won't be in the playoffs.

From *Problem-Solving Training*, by K. Parker, R. Calame, K. K. Gundersen, A. Simon, J. Choi, & M. Amendola, © 2013, Champaign, IL: Research Press (800-519-2707, www.researchpress.com).

Problem-Solving Worksheet 4: Gathering Information

Name _____ Date _____

Describe a problem you have or have had lately.

What is the problem?

_____

_____

What are your **Problem Signs?**

Physical: _____

Emotional: _____

When should you take a deep breath and **Stop and Think?** _____

Circle the **Thinking Error(s):**

    Self-Centered

    Minimizing

    Blaming Others

    Assuming the Worst

    Expecting Hostility

Problem Identification

What is my goal? _____

What is it I don't like? _____

What are the obstacle(s)? _____

What change do I need to make? _____

Gathering Information

What could/did I learn for myself? _____

What could/did I learn from others? _____

From *Problem-Solving Training,* by K. Parker, R. Calame, K. K. Gundersen, A. Simon, J. Choi, & M. Amendola,
© 2013, Champaign, IL: Research Press (800-519-2707, www.researchpress.com).

SESSION 6
Brainstorming Alternatives

RATIONALE

After the gathering information process, the task of generating possible solutions follows. This is the means to respond to the "What do I need to change?" question. Brainstorming as many ideas for solutions to a problem as possible results in a greater likelihood of identifying useful ideas. As D'Zurilla and Goldfield (1971) note, "The more response alternatives a person can generate, the more likely s/he is to arrive at the potentially best ideas for a solution" (p. 114).

MATERIALS

Flip chart (a separate page for each participant)

Problem-Solving Worksheet 5

SESSION PLAN

Introduction and Review

1. Review the group rules and lead an icebreaker.

2. Have group members go over their Problem-Solving Worksheets. Using their own personal scenarios, have them describe their problem and identify their Problem Signs. Then proceed with Stop and Think, Thinking Errors, Problem Identification, and Gathering Information.

3. Referring to the Problem-Solving poster or worksheet, review the steps learned to date, using an example relevant to participants and model each step using self-talk.

Introduce Brainstorming Alternatives

1. Have each youth present a problem, consisting of the problem, the goal, the obstacles, and all other information to be considered. Write these on the flip chart, using a separate page for each youth.

2. Ask the group to make as many suggestions as they can for possible solutions to each of the problems, noting that this is called *brainstorming*. In brainstorming, more ideas lead to better solutions. Emphasis should be placed on creativity, and ideas should flow without judgment. Allowing group members to share a multitude of choices facilitates thinking "outside the box" or beyond their usual repertoire. These

ideas should include strategies for implementation, however, in order to keep the solutions based in reality. Record these on the flip chart and add any other appropriate solutions that the group does not mention. (Keep all flip chart material for the next session.)

Role-Playing

1. Model a problem situation (with your co-facilitator, if necessary). Use a situation relevant to the group or, if need be, one of the following examples from Situation 1, 2, or 3. Ask and answer the following questions:

   - What is the problem?
   - What are the Problem Signs?
   - When should I take a deep breath and Stop and Think?
   - What are the Thinking Error(s)?
   - What is my goal?
   - What are the obstacle(s)?
   - What change do I need to make?
   - What information can I gather from myself? From others?
   - What different options can I brainstorm to solve this problem?

Situation 1

You transferred schools due to some gang members pressuring you to sell drugs for them. Your grades suffered through all of this. On arrival at your new school, you studied really hard for your final history exam and you know you did well. You are called to the office and accused of cheating on the exam. You are told that the people in the next two seats had the same multiple-choice answers. You were sitting next to the wall, and you know that you didn't cheat. You are new in the school, your grades were poor prior to the transfer, and neither the teachers nor students know you. You are convinced somebody's out to get you.

Situation 2

It is Friday, October 1, and you are leaving school to take the 35-minute bus ride home. It's 4 o'clock when you get on the bus and are faced with a tired and grumpy bus driver who has been working all day. This is his final run, and he's in a bad mood. You show him your bus pass and he grumbles, "Sorry. It's expired, you can't get on!" You are sure there's no way he'll help you out. You thought there were 31 days in September and had one more day to buy a new one.

Situation 3

You and your little brother were placed in foster care because your father died and your mom began to abuse drugs heavily after his death. Your mom is not getting better, and your brother feels like you have only each other. Your foster parents are really nice, and you really like them. They like you, too, but were only really prepared to foster one child. Your little brother has always been a real handful, and more so now that he's in foster care. Last night, you overheard your foster parents talking in the kitchen about your brother, and your foster dad said, "I'm not going to accept any more of his rudeness and disrespect. That's it, I'm finished! I'm calling the social worker in the morning." You think to yourself, "They're going to send him away and separate us."

2. Using examples from their Problem-Solving Worksheets, have participants role-play:

> *Problem Signs + Stop and Think + Problem Identification + Thinking Errors + Gathering Information (Own and Others' Perspective) + Brainstorming Alternatives*

3. Conduct performance feedback in the prescribed order: coactor, observers, facilitator(s), and main actor.

Session Review and Practice

1. Briefly review the main points of the session and answer any questions.

2. Hand out the new Problem-Solving Worksheet, to be added to participants' personal journals.

Problem-Solving Worksheet 5: Brainstorming Alternatives

Name _____ Date _____

Describe a problem you have or have had lately.

What is the problem?

_____

_____

What are your **Problem Signs?**

Physical: _____

Emotional: _____

When should you take a deep breath and **Stop and Think?** _____

Circle the **Thinking Error(s):**

    Self-Centered

    Minimizing

    Blaming Others

    Assuming the Worst

    Expecting Hostility

Problem Identification

What is my goal? _____

What is it I don't like? _____

What are the obstacle(s)? _____

What change do I need to make? _____

Gathering Information

What could/did I learn for myself? _____

What could/did I learn from others? _____

Brainstorming Alternatives

Suggest at least three solutions.

_____

_____

_____

From *Problem-Solving Training*, by K. Parker, R. Calame, K. K. Gundersen, A. Simon, J. Choi, & M. Amendola, © 2013, Champaign, IL: Research Press (800-519-2707, www.researchpress.com).

SESSION 7

Evaluating Consequences and Outcomes

RATIONALE

Effective problem solving does not stop at brainstorming solutions but includes a process of reviewing and examining potential consequences of these strategies and their outcomes. Deciding which solution is best involves the use of consequential thinking, in evaluating the relative strengths and weaknesses of the available alternatives (Goldstein, 1999). Participants who have been taught to use "if-then" statements as part of thinking ahead in Anger Control Training can quickly identify with this kind of thinking.

MATERIALS

Flip chart pages from Session 6

Problem-Solving Worksheet 6

Flip chart or whiteboard

SESSION PLAN

Introduction and Review

1. Review the group rules and lead an icebreaker.

2. Have participants go over their Problem-Solving Worksheets. Have them use their own personal scenarios to describe their problem and identify their Problem Signs. Then proceed with Stop and Think, Thinking Errors, Problem Identification, Gathering Information, and Brainstorming Alternatives.

3. Referring to the Problem-Solving poster or worksheet, review the steps learned to date, using an example relevant to participants and model each step using self-talk.

Evaluating Consequences and Outcomes

1. Stress that learning how to figure out what will happen when we choose to do something gives us power over what happens to us. There are different consequences for different behaviors. Discuss with the group the consequences of two

behaviors, one negative and one positive. (For example, when a police officer stops you, you are rude or sarcastic, or you are calm and cooperative.)

2. Have the group look at the flip chart pages from the group's Brainstorming Alternatives session and ask them to evaluate each choice as to what the outcome of those choices might be. Use the concept of the worst and best consequences or pros and cons of each alternative. Model the evaluation process with inner thoughts and questions: "If I do this, what is the worst that can happen? What is likely to happen?" If they have trouble, ask them to guess what the outcome could be. Some of the proposed solutions may be dark or disturbing. However, being open to the reality of the participants' ideas allows them to be reviewed and evaluated by their peers and group facilitators. Gaining others' perspectives is a great addition over the limitations of their own thoughts. Encourage the group to consider which ideas best address the goal without creating more problems that will need to be solved later. It is important to remember that focus should not be placed on the ideas alone, but also on the impact these choices may have on their lives and those of others.

3. Have participants pick their best solution.

4. Have the problem-owner consult the list, make a choice that is best for him or her, and implement it. Have the problem-owner report back to the group in the following session with the consequences/outcome experienced.

5. Bring the lists to the next session.

Role-Playing

1. Model a problem situation (with your co-facilitator, if necessary). Use a situation relevant to the group or, if need be, one of the following examples. Ask and answer the following questions:
   - What is the problem?
   - What are the Problem Signs?
   - When should I take a deep breath and Stop and Think?
   - What are the Thinking Error(s)?
   - What is my goal?
   - What are the obstacle(s)?
   - What change do I need to make?
   - What information can I gather from myself? From others?
   - What alternatives can I brainstorm to solve this problem?
   - Which alternatives will work? Which will not?
   - Which alternative do I choose?

Situation 1

Sometimes when Marla's dad gets really mad, he hits her mom and yells really loudly. It seems like they always argue, but her mom never hits her dad. He's much bigger and meaner, and Marla ends up helping her mom in the end, getting her ice for a swollen eye or a bandage for her cuts. This seems like a lot for a kid to handle, but Marla is an only child and her mom doesn't seem to have that many friends. Marla is always the one she asks for help after her dad storms out of the house and drives away to "cool off." Marla is getting worried that her dad might hit her, too, but nobody will believe her story because they look like such a nice family and they have a lot of money. (Goldstein, 1999, p. 566)

Situation 2

Lately Nina has noticed that her friend Felicia only picks at her lunch at school. Felicia's parents have been putting a lot of pressure on her to bring up her marks. As well, she has been doing a lot more sports and has been jogging for an hour every day. Nina finds that her friend is much more moody and is looking quite thin. She is worried that Felicia is becoming anorexic.

Situation 3

You are at a party, and all of your friends are smoking weed. They ask you to smoke with them. You used to get high a lot, skip school, and not respect any of your parent's rules. You ended up in a treatment center and now must report to a counselor every week. The counselor and your parents have been giving you random drug tests.

2. Using examples from their Problem-Solving Worksheets, have participants role-play:

> *Problem Signs + Stop and Think + Problem Identification + Thinking Errors + Gathering Information (Own and Others' Perspective) + Brainstorming Alternatives + Evaluating Consequences and Outcomes*

3. Conduct performance feedback in the prescribed order: coactor, observers, facilitator(s), and main actor.

Session Review and Homework

1. Briefly review the main points of the session and answer any questions.

2. Hand out the new Problem-Solving Worksheet. At this point, brainstorming and selecting solutions is over. It is now time to have the youth put into motion the process they've selected to respond to their problem. Encourage them to try out their selected solution before the next session and to evaluate how the process worked. Have them fill out this section of their Problem-Solving Worksheet and report back to the group.

Problem-Solving Worksheet 6: Evaluating Consequences and Outcomes

Name _____ Date _____

Describe a probem you have or have had lately.

What is the problem? _____

_____

What are your **Problem Signs?**

Physical: _____

Emotional: _____

When should you take a deep breath and **Stop and Think?** _____

Circle the **Thinking Error(s):**

Self-Centered	Assuming the Worst	Blaming Others
Minimizing	Expecting Hostility	

Problem Identification

What is my goal? _____

What is it I don't like? _____

What are the obstacle(s)? _____

What change do I need to make? _____

Gathering Information

What could/did I learn for myself? _____

What could/did I learn from others? _____

Brainstorming Alternatives

Suggest at least three solutions.

_____   _____

_____   _____

Evaluating Consequences and Outcomes

Circle the alternative above that you think will work best.

Why will it work? _____

Which alternatives will not work? Why not? _____

_____

After you try it, how well did the alternative work? *(Circle one.)*

        Poorly   Not so well   OK   Good   Great

From *Problem-Solving Training,* by K. Parker, R. Calame, K. K. Gundersen, A. Simon, J. Choi, & M. Amendola,
© 2013, Champaign, IL: Research Press (800-519-2707, www.researchpress.com).

SESSION 8

Problem-Solving Practice: I Can Do It!

We are what we repeatedly do. Excellence, then, is not an act, but a habit.
—*Aristotle*

RATIONALE

As McGinnis and Goldstein (1997) observe, "Transfer of training has been shown to be enhanced by implementing procedures which maximize overlearning or response availability. . . . That is, the more we have practiced responses (especially correct ones), the easier it will be to use them in other contexts or at later times" (p. 208). Through repetition of the process of finding and implementing solutions to a variety of problems, participants increase their coping repertoires. This session can be repeated numerous times, in a group setting or individually. Repetition is the best form of emphasis.

MATERIALS

Flip chart or whiteboard

Full Problem-Solving Sequence Worksheet

Flip chart sheets from Sessions 6 and 7

SESSION PLAN

Introduction and Review

1. Review the group rules and lead an icebreaker.

2. Post the flip chart sheets from Sessions 6 and 7. Review what happened when group members tried their chosen alternatives. If they did not get the results they were looking for, what other alternative did they/might they try?

3. Have participants go over their Problem-Solving Worksheets. Using their own personal scenarios, have them describe their problem and identify their Problem Signs. Then proceed with Stop and Think, Thinking Errors, Problem Identification, the information they gathered, the alternative solutions they came up with, and their potential consequences and/or outcomes, and review what happened

when they tried their chosen alternative. If they did not get the results they were looking for, what other alternative did they/might they try?

4. Referring to the Problem-Solving poster or worksheet, review the steps learned to date, using an example relevant to participants and model each step using self-talk.

5. Regardless of our teaching, there are times youth will fail to solve their problems. They may not have properly identified the problem, gathered enough information, or brainstormed a sufficient number of solutions. There are also times when a problem has no solution. What do they do then? To illustrate this to the group, take a new monetary note (e.g., a five-dollar bill). Hold it up vertically from one end. Offer to give the money to anyone who can catch it. Ask a volunteer to stretch index finger and thumb wide apart, both digits halfway up either side of the bill. The volunteer tries to catch it with his or her two fingers after it is released by the holder.

> *This activity is frustrating because it looks simple yet is next to impossible. It illustrates that certain things are beyond a normal person's capabilities, no matter how easy the task may seem. So what does one do? Give up? Yes and no: Yes, because the effort does not match the potential reward. No, because you need to find another way to resolve the problem. Or you may choose to simply move on.*

Role-Playing

1. Model a problem situation (with your co-facilitator, if necessary). Use a situation relevant to the group or, if need be, one of the following examples. Ask and answer the following questions:

   - What is the problem?
   - What are the Problem Signs?
   - When should I take a deep breath and Stop and Think?
   - What are the Thinking Error(s)?
   - What is my goal?
   - What are the obstacle(s)?
   - What change do I need to make?
   - What information can I gather from myself? From others?
   - What alternatives can I brainstorm to solve this problem?
   - Which alternatives will work? Which will not?
   - After you have tried it, how well did the alternative work?

Situation 1

You are traveling by bus to visit a friend you met at camp. He (or she) lives in the heart of a large city. You are following the directions carefully and successfully transfer on to your last bus. This last ride should take 20 minutes. It's 9:00 p.m., and it's getting dark. You are traveling alone with your knapsack and wearing your new designer jacket. Fifteen minutes later, the bus driver pulls the bus over and says, "End of the line. Everybody out!" You get off the bus and start checking out the area and the bus driver pulls away. You should be at 124th Street and Brown Avenue. You look up at the street signs, and you are on the corner of Lincoln and Center Street. Uh-oh! You pull your cell phone out of your backpack to call your friend and remember that it's dead. You say to yourself, "Oh, no! I was going to charge it, but I forgot. Now what do I do? I don't know where I am, and I'll probably get mugged." Just then you hear behind you "Oooh, look at that brand new jacket. I'd love one of those!" You see three figures walking toward you.

Situation 2

As far back as you can remember, you have known that you were adopted. Your parents have always treated you the exact same way they treat your older brother and sister, their biological children. They are good parents but more strict than those of your friends. You are getting pretty fed up with their rules: not being allowed out during the week and always being the one with the earliest curfew on weekends. You and your parents are arguing a lot these days, and your brother and sister are taking their side. It's really not great living at home. You are nearly 16 years old and want to meet your birth parents. They may be in a better situation now and might even consider having you live with them. Your parents wouldn't really miss you, anyways.

Situation 3

You are with a few friends at the park one Saturday night, with nothing much to do. It is getting cold, so you invite everyone back to your house. There isn't anything interesting on television, so you all decide to go onto your chat line on the computer. One of the people online used to be your friend, but you got into a big argument a week ago. Rumors were going around that you and she had alcohol at the school dance. The chaperones couldn't prove it, but the dance ended early because of it. You suspected this person was pretending to be drunk just to show off. Now lots of the students blame you for spoiling their night. One of your friends says, "Why don't we teach this girl a lesson? She pretended to be drunk, so why don't we all make her life miserable by spreading rumors on the Internet that she likes to get drunk and sleep around?" You do not think that this is a good idea and do not want any part of it.

2. Using examples from their Problem-Solving Worksheets, have participants role-play the full problem-solving sequence from start to finish, including assessment of how well the alternative worked:

> *Problem Signs + Stop and Think + Problem Identification + Thinking Errors + Gathering Information (Own and Others' Perspective) + Brainstorming Alternatives + Evaluating Consequences and Outcomes*

3. Conduct performance feedback in the prescribed order: coactor, observers, facilitator(s), and main actor.

Session Review and Practice

1. Briefly review the main points of the session and answer any questions.

2. Hand out copies of the Full Problem-Solving Sequence Worksheet and encourage participants to continue using it to help them organize their thinking anytime they have a problem.

Full Problem-Solving Sequence Worksheet

Name _____ Date _____

Describe a probem you have or have had lately.

What is the problem? _____

_____

What are your **Problem Signs?**

Physical: _____

Emotional: _____

When should you take a deep breath and **Stop and Think?** _____

Circle the **Thinking Error(s):**

Self-Centered   Assuming the Worst   Blaming Others

Minimizing   Expecting Hostility

Problem Identification

What is my goal? _____

What is it I don't like? _____

What are the obstacle(s)? _____

What change do I need to make? _____

Gathering Information

What could/did I learn for myself? _____

What could/did I learn from others? _____

Brainstorming Alternatives

Suggest at least three solutions.

_____   _____

_____   _____

Evaluating Consequences and Outcomes

Circle the alternative above that you think will work best.

Why will it work? _____

Which alternatives will not work? Why not? _____

_____

After you try it, how well did the alternative work? *(Circle one.)*

            Poorly   Not so well   OK   Good   Great

From *Problem-Solving Training,* by K. Parker, R. Calame, K. K. Gundersen, A. Simon, J. Choi, & M. Amendola,
© 2013, Champaign, IL: Research Press (800-519-2707, www.researchpress.com).

Appendix A

Problem-Solving Situations for Children Ages 8 to 12

PROBLEM SIGNS, STOP AND THINK, AND THINKING ERRORS

1. You are next in line for a turn on the swing and someone jumps in and takes the swing first. You say to yourself, "It is the teacher's fault. She never watches." What is the problem? What are your Problem Signs? When should you Stop and Think? Is there a Thinking Error?

2. While carrying your lunch tray, someone bumps into you, and your milk spills all over your meal. You think to yourself, "He must have done it on purpose." What is the problem? What are your Problem Signs? When should you Stop and Think? Is there a Thinking Error?

3. You are in a hurry to meet with your friends and discover that your bike has a flat tire. You are sure they won't wait for you. What is the problem? What are your Problem Signs? When should you Stop and Think? Is there a Thinking Error?

PROBLEM IDENTIFICATION

1. During soccer games, Jon always takes the ball up the field by himself and never passes. Most of the time, the other team takes the ball off him before he can score. His coach has warned him that he will sit on the bench if he cannot be a team player. Jon feels this is unfair because other team members do the same thing. What is the problem? What are Jon's Problem Signs? When should he Stop and Think? Is there a Thinking Error? What is his goal? What is the obstacle? What change needs to be made?

2. Sarah often butts into conversations that her friends are having. Lately she has noticed that they turn away from her when they see her approaching. She doesn't know what their problem is; she just wants to be a part of the group. What is the problem? What are Sarah's Problem Signs? When should she Stop and Think? Is there a Thinking Error? What is her goal? What is the obstacle? What change needs to be made?

3. Maria and Carl both have chores to do around the house. Carl always does his, but Maria often avoids doing hers. This week, when it is time to get their allowance, Carl gets his, but Maria doesn't. Maria thinks her parents love Carl more. What is

the problem? What are Maria's Problem Signs? When should she Stop and Think? Is there a Thinking Error? What is her goal? What is the obstacle? What change needs to be made?

GATHERING INFORMATION

1. You were given some math homework to do and forgot your assignment book at school. You cannot remember what pages you need to do, but your neighbor is in the same class and would know. Your math teacher is strict and will check your homework. You are pretty good at subtraction, so you could probably get it done before school starts tomorrow. What is the problem? What are your Problem Signs? When should you Stop and Think? Is there a Thinking Error? What is your goal? What is the obstacle? What change needs to be made? What information can you gather from yourself? From others?

2. You want to go to the store to buy some playing cards. You are not allowed to go there on your own. Your brother comes in the house to tell your mom that he is bicycling to the store with his friends. You ask if you can come along, and he says, "No, we don't want a little kid hanging around with us." As usual, your mom says nothing. What is the problem? What are your Problem Signs? When should you Stop and Think? Is there a Thinking Error? What is your goal? What is the obstacle? What change needs to be made? What information can you gather from yourself? From others?

3. You have not been doing very well in school. Your parents have said that, if you improve, you can choose to do a special activity, within reason. You have just brought home your report card and have done very well. You must now decide whether to ask to go bungee jumping or horseback riding, or to a scary movie. What is the problem? What are your Problem Signs? When should you Stop and Think? Is there a Thinking Error? What is your goal? What is the obstacle? What change needs to be made? What information can you gather from yourself? From others?

BRAINSTORMING ALTERNATIVES

1. Your dad is a mechanic and has his garage next to your house. He always works until 5:30 and doesn't like to be disturbed. You have been invited to a friend's house after school to shoot some hoops. If you walk there, you will be too tired to play. What is the problem? What are your Problem Signs? When should you Stop and Think? Is there a Thinking Error? What is your goal? What is the obstacle? What change needs to be made? What information can you gather from yourself? From others? What alternatives can you brainstorm to solve this problem?

2. Your sister loaned you her favorite bracelet and made you swear you would take good care of it. So that it would not break, you took it off before gym class and left it on the bench. After class, you dressed quickly because the bell had already rung and you have to catch your bus. Once you get home, your sister asks for her bracelet back, and you realize you forgot to put it back on. What is the problem? What are your Problem Signs? When should you Stop and Think? Is there a Thinking Error? What is your goal? What is the obstacle? What change needs to be made?

What information can you gather from yourself? From others? What alternatives can you brainstorm to solve this problem?

3. You come home at 5:00 and are really hungry. Usually, you can smell supper cooking and know that food will soon be on the table. Today, you don't smell anything. You say to yourself, "What the heck, I need to eat!" A few minutes later, you hear your mother and dad talking quietly in the living room. What is the problem? What are your Problem Signs? When should you Stop and Think? Is there a Thinking Error? What is your goal? What is the obstacle? What change needs to be made? What information can you gather from yourself? From others? What alternatives can you brainstorm to solve this problem?

EVALUATING CONSEQUENCES AND OUTCOMES

1. You and your friends have been skateboarding all summer. Often you board in the park, but once in a while you go to the top of this very steep hill and talk about how exciting it would be to board down it. You know that it is dangerous. If you even hit one rock . . . It's the end of the summer, and all your friends dare each other to do it. What is the problem? What are your Problem Signs? When should you Stop and Think? Is there a Thinking Error? What is your goal? What is the obstacle? What change needs to be made? What information can you gather from yourself? From others? What alternatives can you brainstorm to solve this problem? What would be the consequences/outcomes of each alternative? Which one is best for you?

2. You have just moved to a new town and do not know anybody. There is a park down the street with a basketball hoop. You aren't too bad a player and think you may be able to meet people if you take your ball and start practicing your foul shots. After you have been there for awhile, some kids come along to watch you. The ball gets away from you, and one of the bigger kids takes it. The bigger kids start passing it back and forth, over your head, so you can't get it back. What is the problem? What are your Problem Signs? When should you Stop and Think? Is there a Thinking Error? What is your goal? What is the obstacle? What change needs to be made? What information can you gather from yourself? From others? What alternatives can you brainstorm to solve this problem? What would be the consequences/outcomes of each alternative? Which one is best for you?

3. Last weekend you went on a sleepover at your friend's. Your best friend does not get along with this girl and now is mad at you. You have tried talking to your best friend, but she does not want to listen. Your birthday party is in two weeks and you want to invite them both. What is the problem? What are your Problem Signs? When should you Stop and Think? Is there a Thinking Error? What is your goal? What is the obstacle? What change needs to be made? What information can you gather from yourself? From others? What alternatives can you brainstorm to solve this problem? What would be the consequences/outcomes of each alternative? Which one is best for you?

Appendix B
Supplementary Activities

Interactive Activities

STEP 1: PROBLEM SIGNS

Getting people to recognize the physical and emotional cues that they are encountering a problem situation is a worthwhile skill to teach. This exercise may be used on its own; however, it is also an excellent opportunity to emphasize the importance of considering the emotional condition of self and others when problem solving.

Have participants think of different emotions they might experience when encountering a problem. In order to do this, they may need to be prompted with sample situations like the following:

1. It is nighttime, and you are going to visit someone for the first time. You believe you are on the right bus but, at the end of the line, you are let off alone in a strange neighborhood. You see none of the landmarks you were supposed to look for.

2. You are not going to make your curfew again. You try to call home, but your cell phone is out of power and there are no pay phones around. You have been warned that the next time this happened you would be grounded for a month, and you have front row tickets to a concert next week.

Have participants write their emotions down on a piece of paper and create their own lists of feeling words. Doing so contributes to building a greater feelings vocabulary. Once participants have done this individually, ask them to share their lists with the group and have a collective discussion on how each of these emotions can be expressed in the body. If appropriate, explain that these body signals are much like the cues discussed in the Prepare Curriculum's Anger Control Training. Recognizing these physical and emotional cues helps them realize they have a problem.

STEP 2: STOP AND THINK

Puzzles are an excellent tool to emphasize taking the time to stop and think before reacting or trying to solve a problem. This brings a more concrete and practical illustration of the Stop and Think concept to the session.

A trip to a game or magic store can provide you with small jigsaw puzzles, three-dimensional puzzles, interlocking metal rings, and so forth. Give participants the opportunity to use the puzzles to learn that being organized and planning ahead can provide faster and more successful solutions.

STEP 3: PROBLEM IDENTIFICATION

Participants may more easily understand the concepts of goals, obstacles, and changes needed if they first look at problems that are not their own. Using newspaper articles or popular movies, have participants examine the stories to identify underlying goals and obstacles. Ask whether the person remained on track toward achieving the goal or became derailed by obstacles. Discuss with the group what changes the person might need to make in order to reach the goal.

By doing this exercise first, participants can more easily apply the formula "goals, obstacles, and changes needed" to their personal problem situations. This exercise clearly illustrates this step of the problem-solving process.

STEP 4: GATHERING INFORMATION

Own Perspective

Have participants look at a picture that is visually ambiguous (i.e., can be seen in more than one way). Each individual will see the picture in his or her own way. One image, or the other, will be predominant. Which image the group members deem predominant can be used to illustrate gathering information from their own perspective. In the example provided, some people will first see the image of an Inuit in a snow parka looking into a dark area; others will first see a person's profile. In some cases, individuals have trouble seeing the second image, even when it is pointed out to them. Many other examples of this type are available on the Internet under "optical illusions."

By using an exercise like this to begin a session, facilitators direct participants to consider how perspective plays a role in the way problem situations are resolved. They may have to look at their problem from more than one angle. The exercise also underlines the importance of taking enough time to gather all possible information. Others' perspectives can be realistic and worthy of consideration, too.

Others' Perspective

There are many creative ways to illustrate the differences in what other people see and/or think. "Twenty Questions" games or brainteasers require listening and appreciation of others' perspectives. Each person's different point of view and insight, when considered collectively, aids the group members in discovering the answer.

The board game Clue, by Parker Brothers, is a well-known problem-solving game. It requires participants to gather information: from their own cards (own perspective) and from those of their opponents. They also gather information (others' perspective) by observing other players' lines of questioning, movements around the game board, and nonverbal cues.

STEP 5: BRAINSTORMING ALTERNATIVES

Road Trip

In this activity, the group is divided into pairs and each pair is given a map. Each pair is given the same destination and starting point and is asked to plan the route. Each pair, however, is given different extra elements to incorporate into the plan (e.g., construction detours, weather conditions, vehicle abilities).

If the group seems to be adept at these challenges, adding more elements (some important, some irrelevant) can make the process more interesting. You can also ask the pair to first develop a route and then add elements or obstacles that force them to reroute.

Have the groups compare routes afterward and discuss the different ideas each group went through before deciding on a final route.

One-Act Play

Have the youth act out a role-play, stopping before the end. The observers predict what will happen and brainstorm alternative endings. The actors then continue to play out their scene, using each of the alternative endings, and then the observers give feedback.

STEP 6: EVALUATING CONSEQUENCES AND OUTCOMES

A successful strategy for teaching evaluating consequences and outcomes involves using videos or stories.

Critic

Show the group a film in which the main character has to make some critical choices or decisions. Ask the group to look for times this happens as they watch. Once the film is over, ask the group to identify the main character's choices and how these choices impacted the story's ending. An example is the film *Changing Lanes,* starring Ben Affleck and Samuel L. Jackson. The group can evaluate the consequences and outcomes of the two main character's actions: Doyle Gibson decides to return a valuable legal file—as a recovering alcoholic he chooses not to drink, as a father he chooses to persevere for the sake of his children. Gavin Banek decides not to give Gibson a ride after the accident—he chooses to tamper with Gibson's bank account and to expose the law firm's plans to control a trust fund. Ask the group to speculate on the new endings the film would have if the characters made different decisions. If time allows, have participants write a new ending to the film, starting by changing the decision one of the main characters makes.

Choose-an-Ending Story

Read the beginning of a story and leave the end to the imagination of the group. Depending on the individual versus group choice of the story's ending, the development and outcomes change. There are many Internet sites on which youth can read stories, choose different endings, and examine their outcomes (for example, www.infinite-story.com).

The Director

View video clips or films and pause the action to have the youth predict the next scene. For a younger group, discuss the story of the Three Little Pigs and how each pig's choice of building material led to a different outcome. By evaluating the outcomes of these choices, the group can learn that a better choice of building material would get a better result the next time.

Sudoku

The rapidly growing international pastime of Sudoku has much to offer in the development of problem-solving skills. Sudoku is a number placement puzzle that includes a grid with 81 squares. Some numbers in the puzzle are filled in, and the solver of the puzzle must fill in the rest. In each of nine 3 x 3 sections, the numbers 1 through 9 must appear only once. The problem solver must arrange the 81 spaces in the nine rows and nine columns so that all the numbers between 1 and 9 also appear without repeating. Once that task is completed, the problem is solved.

Sudoku can help participants develop different parts of the problem-solving process. For example, inserting a number onto the grid requires brainstorming alternatives and selecting one. The selection of one alternative results in the problem-solving step of evaluating possible outcomes. The process itself requires the problem solver to think laterally, in a means-end way, using causal, consequential, and alternative solution thinking.

A sample Sudoku puzzle and its solution follow; numerous other examples are available on the Internet.

Sudoku Puzzle

4	1			7			3	2
	2		1					6
	7	6	9		3	8		
	8		5				6	
6	9						8	3
	3				6		7	
		3	2		8	1	4	
1					9		2	
8	6			4			9	5

Sudoku Puzzle Solution

4	1	8	6	7	5	9	3	2
3	2	9	1	8	4	7	5	6
5	7	6	9	2	3	8	1	4
7	8	1	5	3	2	4	6	9
6	9	5	4	1	7	2	8	3
2	3	4	8	9	6	5	7	1
9	5	3	2	6	8	1	4	7
1	4	7	3	5	9	6	2	8
8	6	2	7	4	1	3	9	5

Cooperative Games

Cooperative games may be used as an introduction to problem-solving sessions. The emphasis on cooperative games is to make sure that all participants are involved in decision making. To this end, the facilitators must encourage input from all group members and be "vigilant protectors," ensuring that everyone's ideas are respected. The facilitator can then refer to events that occurred during the challenge to illustrate the points being taught in the session.

STEP 1: PROBLEM SIGNS

Puzzles

Materials: 20- to 50-piece puzzles, depending on the age of the participants (one puzzle per pair of participants)

Divide the group or have youth divide into pairs and have them sit at a desk or table. Give each pair a bag with a puzzle in it but without the picture of the completed puzzle. Have youth put the puzzle together. Note the physical and emotional cues the youth might be exhibiting as they have trouble putting the puzzle together. After five minutes, stop the activity to ask each group member what his or her physical and emotional cues are. Next give them the picture (or box) of their puzzle to use. Note how much easier it is to do the puzzle now. Refer to these differences and the cues noticed in the lesson. It is much easier to solve problems with help.

STEP 2: STOP AND THINK

Scavenger Hunt

Choose five to eight places within a reasonable distance of your training room. Create clues that would describe each place and write each on a piece of paper. Lay out a route from one place to the next and number each place. Ideally, the places chosen should maximize your space so participants have to move around and think. Place the clue for place 2 at place 1, place 3 at place 2, and so forth. Place a prize of some kind for the group to find at the last place. For example:

Clue 1: It's been a slice!

Clue 2: (Placed under the edge of a toaster) I can be turned on from near or far.

Clue 3: (Placed by a television) I may often look dirty, but the smells that come from me are good enough to eat.

Clue 4: (Prize, placed in a barbeque grill)

When the group has found the prize, ask them how it felt when they needed to become detectives, read each clue, stop and think, and so on.

STEP 3: PROBLEM IDENTIFICATION

Saving the Village

Materials: Large empty soda pop bottle, two 30-foot ropes, hangers, string, pieces of wood, paper clips, elastic bands, etc.

Context

You are members of a nomadic, agricultural settlement that have moved to a new sight because the soil was depleted at the old site. You have set up your new homes and planted your crops. You are now ready to make a flower garden in the center of the village, but you come across a bomb buried in the earth.

Method

Make a large circle on the ground with one of the ropes to form a barrier. Fill the bottle with water and put the cap on very loosely. Place the bottle in the middle of the circle. Read the story above and tell the group that the bottle is really a bomb. They must remove it from the circle without crossing the rope barrier and without touching the bottle with their hands or spilling the liquid, as this will detonate the bomb. They may use any of the tools provided. (One solution: Two people take the ends of the other rope and, walking around the bottle, wrap the rope around its neck and move to 180 degrees of each other. Pulling the rope taut, they then lift the bottle and move it out of the circle together.)

Ask the following questions and discuss: What was the goal in this challenge? What were the problems faced in reaching this goal? Was the rope circle an obstacle? What else was an obstacle?

STEP 4: GATHERING INFORMATION

Own Perspective

Riddles

Read out a riddle and have the group members try to find the answer by asking only questions that can be answered yes or no. Examples:

1. I have many feathers to help me fly. I have a body and head, but I'm not alive. It is your strength that determines how far I go. You can hold me in your hand, but I'm never thrown. What am I? (Answer: An arrow.)

2. Two men are in a desert. They both have backpacks on. One of the men is dead. The man who is alive has his pack open, but the dead man's pack is closed. What is in the pack? (Answer: A parachute that didn't open.)

3. A man was outside taking a walk when it began to rain. He did not have an umbrella, and he wasn't wearing a hat. His clothes were soaked, yet not a single hair on his head got wet. How could this happen? (Answer: He was bald.)

Discuss the following questions: What different thoughts did the participants have when they were trying to solve the riddle? What parts of the riddle were facts? What parts were their opinions?

Others' Perspective

Bear Traps

Materials: 20 discs/squares of four different colors (may be cardboard, plastic, vinyl)

Context

You are a group of campers and have pitched your tents next to a farmer's field. He is happy to have you there but warns you to be careful of the bear traps he has placed in the field to protect his berry patch. You are welcome, however, to go pick some berries for your supper.

Method

Lay the discs/squares out over an area far enough apart to be reached by a stride. On a piece of paper, map out which discs are "traps." Read the story above and have the group line up. Tell them that they are going berry picking but first must cross the field, avoiding the bear traps. Let them know that some discs/squares are live traps and some are not. The first person tries to cross the field. If he or she steps on a trap, clap, have the person go to the back of the line, and have the next person try. The group attempts to remember where the traps are and guide participants through verbally.

Discuss the following questions: Did group members see the benefit of relying on others? Point out that the group might have stepped on many more traps without the advice of the other group members. If each participant has only a little bit of information or relies only on himself or herself, the risk of making a poor choice is greater.

STEP 5: BRAINSTORMING ALTERNATIVES

Lego Structure

Materials: Lego or similar building blocks

Give the group a building project to create together. Have the project be open ended so that group members may discuss and decide on how their structure will look (e.g., a castle, car, boat, skyscraper). Allow time for building.

Discuss how many ideas the group brainstormed before deciding on a structure they could really make. Were all ideas considered carefully?

STEP 6: EVALUATING CONSEQUENCES AND OUTCOMES

Surviving on a Lifeboat

Materials: Paper and pencils

Have the group work in triads or small groups. Give them the following situation: "You are on a sinking ship. You have five minutes to gather 10 items to bring on the lifeboat. What would you bring?" Allow time for groups to compile their lists.

Have participants share their lists with the larger group, explaining why they chose the items they did. Each group may have forgotten something important. By listening to others' opinions and gathering facts for themselves, they evaluate the consequences and outcomes of forgetting these items. Conversely, if they are happy with their lists, they explain why the outcome of their decisions was positive.

Problem-Solving Quest

Facilitators who are well versed in the online game Dungeons and Dragons or similar quest-type games can use the adventure game format as a popular, practical context for teaching the problem-solving procedure and associated prosocial skills. These kinds of quest-type games, whether played on a computer or not, have a broad appeal to youth, especially those slow to warm up to more traditional forms of instruction.

The principles described here, designed for youth ages 8 to 18, illustrate the opportunities that exist. The actual content will vary depending on the individuals running the quest and its participants. Two facilitators, one acting as the Quest Lord and the other providing general assistance, control the direction of the game.

Participants will be selected to play or have opportunity to choose to play from a variety of characters in the game, such as royalty, knights, magicians, heroes, priests, victims, and so forth. All these characters are created by the Quest Lord or facilitator and have specific characteristics, relationships, or personalities relevant to the quest. The beauty of this "do it yourself" model is that any strongly negative or violent characters or problems they might present can be eliminated from the game. Instead, these bad guys or challenges can be overcome adeptly using problem-solving skills (or other ART skills). The Quest Lord controls the issues and moves the group to come up with prosocial responses. When a person uses a power or talent for harm, the Quest Lord can introduce new characters or tools to turn the quest quickly toward the positive. Dice are rolled to reward prosocial responses by perhaps increasing special powers or unveiling new information or tools helpful for being victorious in the quest.

Rather than using guns, spears, or weapons to solve conflicts or surmount obstacles in the Problem-Solving Quest, youth are encouraged to use the tools of problem solving, such as stopping to think when posed with a problem, recognizing the scope of the problem, and anticipating the obstacles that limit problem resolution. They can look carefully at the problem, decide what is fact or opinion and whether or not there are thinking errors, and brainstorm with their peers to propose potential solutions. All this should be done in character, of course, allowing the youth to do or think what the *character* would do without their needing to be loyal to negative peer group values. The options that are chosen to try to solve the problems are likely to include Skillstreaming sequences, Anger Control techniques, and devices for developing empathy as well as

Thanks go to youth care worker Eric Dorais of the Crossroads Residential Treatment Unit of Batshaw Youth and Family Centres, Montreal, for the ideas presented here. To share strategy and expansions and to acquire potential content for additional problem-solving quests, contact him at eric_dorais@ssss.gouv.qc.ca.

moral and ethical values, providing the Quest Lord has a quick sense of vision of how to plan and lead the group.

SAMPLE PROBLEM-SOLVING QUEST SCENARIO

The scene is Loftwich, in the kingdom of Stealthshire, 1601. The good king of Stealthshire has commissioned you, as a faithful subject, to recover and return to him a map. Not just any map, this one leads to the royal treasury hidden in the mountains, three generations before, during a war with the Drunes. The kingdom has experienced seven years of drought and famine, and the people are suffering from a lack of food and medicine.

You are the king's locksmith and have been selected to be a member of the king's delegation, along with three of his most trusted knights, the king's personal magician, and Friar Luck. You are to travel to the end of the kingdom and retrieve the map from a chateau no longer controlled by the king but now inhabited by citizens of the neighboring kingdom. The king has had no contact with his subjects in this part of his kingdom for over six years. In addition, these difficult years have made it impossible to travel far away from Loftwich, so no contact has been made with the neighboring kingdom, Plausland. Plauslandians are thought to be tall, fierce, and greedy and concerned about profit only. Their armies are fierce and strong, but no war has existed between the two countries for over 100 years. The king requires the map to get the hidden gold and treasures for use in trade with faraway countries, where food and medicines are said to be plentiful. The group sets out with adequate provisions for only a few days. Together, as they travel, they need to determine which foods growing wild are safe to eat. They might encounter wilderness survivors in the forest and ask for advice. They are challenged to kill and retrieve a wild boar big enough to feed them for a week that retreats into a deadly poison thicket in the darkness of night. (Again, the Quest Lord can direct the activities to also use Anger Control, Moral Reasoning, Skillstreaming, and other Prepare Curriculum training elements to role-play and change the outcomes.)

When your delegation arrives near the castle, Friar Luck is sent ahead to greet those holding the castle. He is to try to make the delegation welcome enough to gain access to the castle and then be able to retrieve the map. One hour, then two, then three hours pass and still no sign of Friar Luck. No doubt he has been slain.

The delegation approaches the castle and observes fierce-looking armor-clad giants guarding the drawbridge. They have large staff-like objects at their side, and the one who appears to be their leader has a shiny brass-colored pouch attached to his waist. Is the map in the pouch? Where is Friar Luck? What do we do now? How do we get the map?

Perhaps a deal is negotiated with the guards? Perhaps a big distraction can divert the guards' attention while the magician tries to get close enough to visualize the map in the pouch?

Once the map is retrieved, over one session or a dozen sessions of Problem-Solving Quest, a new quest presents itself. Having secured the map, how does the group now retrieve the hidden treasury from the mountains? And so on and so forth.

Appendix C

Problem-Solving Training Fidelity Forms

Problem-Solving Training Facilitator's Evaluation Form

Facilitators _____

Date _____ Session no. _____

	YES	NO	N/A
1. If there were issues from the last session, was a follow-up done?	❏	❏	❏
2. Were the group rules reviewed?	❏	❏	❏
3. Was an icebreaker/activity done?	❏	❏	❏
4. Was the previous session reviewed?	❏	❏	❏
5. Did participants share a problem from their Problem-Solving Worksheet?	❏	❏	❏
6. Was the new problem-solving step introduced?	❏	❏	❏
7. Were visual aids used?	❏	❏	❏
8. Did the facilitators correctly model the problem-solving steps learned to date?	❏	❏	❏
9. Were the steps identified during the modeling?	❏	❏	❏
10. Was the role-play relevant to the participants?	❏	❏	❏
11. Did the participants choose an example of a situation in which they needed to problem-solve?	❏	❏	❏
12. Did each participant correctly role-play as the main actor?	❏	❏	❏
13. Did all participants provide performance feedback?	❏	❏	❏
14. Was the session material reviewed?	❏	❏	❏
15. Were new Problem-Solving Worksheets distributed?	❏	❏	❏
16. Was behavior management an issue during the session?	❏	❏	❏

Comments:

From *Problem-Solving Training*, by K. Parker, R. Calame, K. K. Gundersen, A. Simon, J. Choi, & M. Amendola, © 2013, Champaign, IL: Research Press (800-519-2707, www.researchpress.com).

Problem-Solving Training Observer's Checklist

Facilitators _____

Observer _____ Date _____ Session no. _____

Using the following criteria, please assess how effectively the facilitator and co-facilitator conducted the Problem-Solving Training group.

Scoring

    0 = Not competent

    1 = Mildly competent

    2 = Competent

    3 = Highly competent

1. Demonstrated knowledge of the content presented.	0	1	2	3
2. Kept up an appropriate pace during the presentation.	0	1	2	3
3. Used platform skills (body, hands, eye contact, facial expression, voice).	0	1	2	3
4. Related to participants and kept them interested and involved.	0	1	2	3
5. Used visuals to support the presentation and clarify concepts.	0	1	2	3
6. Conveyed enthusiasm and a belief in what was presented.	0	1	2	3
7. Organized and structured the session (followed established procedure).	0	1	2	3

Observer's feedback and recommendations:

Observer's comments and recommendations received:

_____   _____

(Facilitator signature and date)   *(Co-facilitator signature and date)*

Appendix D

The BART Program: Back-up Aggression Replacement Training for Crisis Intervention

Problem-solving strategies can become central to interventions designed to assist youth who may be acting out by putting themselves or others at risk. One such strategy, the BART program, has been designed by educators for use in residential, correctional, or educational settings. It is intended to help curb acting-out behavior that jeopardizes optimal classroom/unit functioning, students' academic pursuits, and safety of self/others.

Youth who are in crisis after use of violence, illegal substance abuse, serious behavioral disturbances, or running away from school, home, or residential care can be referred to this program as a transition prior to resuming their normal functioning in their usual location. This crisis intervention approach, based on Aggression Replacement Training, is called BART, an acronym for Back-up Aggression Replacement Training.

Upon arrival at the BART treatment site, youth are presented with a program designed to help them reflect on their problems and their resolution. A youth arrives at the alternative site, accompanied by a referring worker, where he or she will spend time working on solutions to any presenting problem(s). The referring worker identifies the problem(s) to be worked on from a list of 24 or more typical problems that often require this type of intervention. The youth is consulted and agrees to the intervention.

Materials

A list of 24 or more typical problems, to be completed by the referring worker

A knapsack

A three-drawer cabinet, containing the following:

Thanks to Kuldip Thind, Faith Fraser, Cathy Millar, Anna Maria Ferro, Bruce Cummings, Michael Smeaton, Daintie Hines, John Carzello, and Mike Bury of the Crossroads Residential Treatment Unit of Batshaw Youth and Family Centres, Montreal, for their innovativeness and willingness to share this idea. Also thanks to Dr. Sara Salmon, PEACE4Kids, Denver, Colorado, for the knapsack activity upon which the BART innovation and intervention is based.

Drawer 1: A total of 24 or more water-filled plastic balls or tennis balls, with a different typical referral problem labeled on each (referral balls).

Drawer 2: Approximately 30 empty plastic balls or air-filled balloons that have Skillstreaming skill names written on them (resource balls).

Drawer 3: Approximately 30 of the same empty plastic balls or air-filled balloons, which are labeled with character traits or virtues that the youth feels he or she possesses or should use to work on the referring problems (resource balls).

The referring worker places the referral balls (Drawer 1) in the knapsack. The youth then chooses the resource balls (Drawers 2 and 3) that he or she wants to use in the knapsack. For the subsequent hours, days, or weeks, the youth will use the skills and character traits chosen to write, role-play, do artwork (drawings, collages), and engage in other exercises designed to focus on developing prosocial skills and competencies to address the situation.

Following is an example of how the BART program works.

Pierre's Case

Pierre is a 12-year-old boy who has assaulted another youth in the hallway at school. The youth has insulted Pierre's family in a mean and inappropriate manner. Pierre attends a junior high school that has a zero tolerance policy for violence in the school. Pierre was warned by the group home where he resides that use of violence to resolve disputes would result in his being referred to a BART site.

The BART program uses a metaphor, as well as the usual paperwork, to admit a youth to the program. The youth is given a knapsack that has the reason(s) for referral written on water-filled plastic ball(s) or tennis ball(s). The referring worker has selected the appropriate balls or balloons for the intervention and placed them in the sack. This represents the burden or baggage a youth is carrying. In Pierre's case, there are three balls: one that represents using violence, another that represents lack of self-control, and still another that represents not respecting rules. When put into the knapsack, the balls have a definite weight which, following the metaphor, the youth must try on to appreciate the weight. The youth should not carry the bag around for any extended period of time.

Pierre selects the Skillstreaming skills of Expressing Your Feelings, Using Self-Control, Keeping Out of Fights, Making a Complaint Constructively, Apologizing, and Negotiating to resolve the issues that brought him to BART. He also chooses to use the character traits of Perseverance, Self-Control, Respect, and Caring (from Peace4Kids) as the character traits useful in resolving his issues.

Reflecting on the events that brought him to BART, Pierre works at resolution by clearly identifying and understanding the presenting problem. Then he proceeds to follow the next steps of problem-solving strategy, which includes gathering information from his own behavior and its origins, as well as from the perspective of the school personnel, the victim of his assault, and Pierre's family, who were insulted.

Pierre then brainstorms about when and where to use the tools he has selected. Pierre decides to Express his Feelings to his group home staff around the hurt and anger he feels from the insult to his family, as well as to convey his disappointment at his use of violence, which resulted in his being sent to the BART site. He will practice the skills of Using Self-Control and Keeping Out of Fights as alternatives to dealing with his feelings in an aggressive way. He will use the skills of Apologizing to the victim for the assault but also use Making a Complaint Constructively to explain that he would appreciate that his victim no longer insult his family. He offers his victim a solution of mutual Respect in the hopes that he will agree.

When this work is done, Pierre is allowed to remove the heavy referral balls (using violence and lack of self-control). He then tries the knapsack back on to feel how his load has been lightened and that his efforts are bringing him closer to returning to his own group home. He has had to use Perseverance and Self-Control in the process and finally shows Caring and Respect for the other youth, his family, and the school by Negotiating to reenter school by promising to respect rules and offering to do a school improvement project to demonstrate his commitment to peaceful school life.

When the knapsack has been emptied of its burdens, because of Pierre's work toward resolving his own problems, Pierre then returns to his normal place of residence and school. The tools he uses are important, but even more important is the problem-solving process he has used to regain control of his own life. Teaching this kind of process can be the most important gift that can be given to a troubled youth because it helps the youth to find and use his or her own abilities to solve his or her own problems.

References

Akhtar, N., & Bradley, E. J. (1991). Social information processing deficits of aggressive children: Present findings and implication for social skills training. *Clinical Psychology Review, 11,* 621–644.

Amidon, E., Roth, J., & Greenberg, M. (1991). *Group magic.* St. Paul, MN: Paul S. Amidon & Associates.

Argyle, M. (1983). *The psychology of interpersonal behaviour* (4th ed.). Harmondsworth, Middlesex, England: Penguin Books.

Argyle, M., & Kendon, A. (1967). The experimental analysis of social performance. In L. Berkowitz (Ed.), *Advances in experimental social psychology* (Vol. 3, pp. 55–97). New York: Academic Press.

Bandura, A. (1977). *Social learning theory.* Englewood Cliffs, NJ: Prentice Hall.

Bandura, A. (1986). *Social foundations of thought and action: A social-cognitive theory.* Englewood Cliffs, NJ: Prentice Hall.

Bellack, A. S., Mueser, K., Gingerich, S., & Agresta, J. (1997). *Social skills training for schizophrenia: A step by step guide.* New York: Guilford.

Brown, P., & Fraser, C. (1979). Speech as a marker of situations. In K. Scherer & H. Giles (Eds.), *Social markers in speech* (pp. 33–62). Cambridge: Cambridge University Press.

Calame, R., & Parker, K. (2013). *Family TIES: A family-based intervention to complement Prepare©, ART©, and TIES youth groups.* Champaign, IL: Research Press.

Chang, E. C., D'Zurilla, T. J., & Sanna, L. J. (2004). *Social problem solving: Theory, research and training.* Washington DC: American Psychological Association.

Crick, N. R., & Dodge, K. A. (1996). Social information-processing mechanisms in reactive and proactive aggression. *Child Development, 67,* 993–1002.

Crutchfield, R. S. (1969). Nurturing the cognitive skills in productive thinking. In *Life skills in school and society.* Washington, DC: Association of Supervision and Curriculum Development.

Davey, L., Day, A., & Howells, K. (2005). Anger, over-control and serious violent offending. *Aggressive and Violent Behaviour, 10,* 624–635.

DiDonato, N. C. (2013). Effective self- and co-regulation in collaborative learning groups: An analysis of how students regulate problem solving of authentic interdisciplinary tasks. *Instructional Science: An International Journal of the Learning Sciences, 41*(1), 25–47.

Dobson, D. J., & Dobson, K. S. (1981). Problem-solving strategies in depressed and non-depressed college students. *Cognitive Therapy and Research, 5,* 237–249.

Dodsworth, P. R. (2002). *Evaluation of a social problem-solving curriculum for preventing early adolescent aggression.* Dissertation Abstracts International: Section B: The Sciences and Engineering, Vol. 63 (5-B), p. 2649.

Dollard, J., & Miller, N. E. (1950). *Personality and psychotherapy.* New York: McGraw-Hill.

D'Zurilla, T. J., & Goldfried, M. R. (1971). Problem solving and behaviour modification. *Journal of Abnormal Psychology, 78*(1), 107–126.

D'Zurilla, T. J., & Nezu, A. M. (1999). *Problem-solving therapy: A social competence approach to clinical intervention.* New York: Springer.

D'Zurilla, T. J., Nezu, A. M., & Maydeu-Olivares, A. (2004). Social problem solving: Theory and assessment. In E. C. Chang, T. J. D'Zurilla, & L. J. Sanna (Eds.), *Social problem solving: Theory, research and training* (pp. 11–15). Washington, DC: American Psychological Association.

Elias, M. J., & Tobias, S. E. (1996). *Social problem solving: Interventions in the schools.* New York: Guilford.

Foster, S. L., Prinz, R. J., & O'Leary, K. D. (1983). Impact of problem-solving communication training and generalization procedures on family conflict. *Child and Family Behavior Therapy, 5,* 1–23.

Friendship, C., Blund, L., Erikson, M., Travers, R., & Thornton, D. M. (2003). Cognitive-behavioral treatment for imprisoned offenders: An evaluation of HM Prison Service's cognitive skills programmes. *Legal and Criminological Psychology, 8,* 103–114.

Frydenberg, E. (1997). *Adolescent coping: Theoretical and research perspectives.* London: Routledge.

Gardner, H. (1993). *Multiple intelligences: The theory in practice.* New York: Basic Books.

Gibbs, J. C. (1993). Moral-cognitive interventions. In A. P. Goldstein & C. R. Huff (Eds.), *The gang intervention handbook* (pp. 159–185). Champaign, IL: Research Press.

Gibbs, J. C. (1996). Sociomoral group treatment for young offenders. In C. R. Hollin & K. Howells (Eds.), *Clinical approaches to working with young offenders* (pp. 129–149). Chichester, England: Wiley.

Gibbs, J. C., Potter, G. B. , & Goldstein, A. P. (1995). *The EQUIP Program: Teaching youth to think and act responsibly through a peer-helping approach.* Champaign, IL: Research Press.

Glick, B., & Gibbs, J. C. (2011). *Aggression Replacement Training: A comprehensive intervention for adolescent youth.* (3rd ed.). Champaign, IL: Research Press.

Goldstein, A. P. (1988). *The Prepare Curriculum: Teaching prosocial competencies.* Champaign, IL: Research Press.

Goldstein, A. P. (1994). *The ecology of aggression.* New York: Plenum.

Goldstein, A. P. (1999). *The Prepare Curriculum: Teaching prosocial competencies* (Rev. ed.). Champaign, IL: Research Press.

Goldstein, A. P. (2004a). ART and beyond: The Prepare Curriculum. In A.P. Goldstein, R. Nensen, B. Daleflod, & M. Kalt (Eds.), *New perspectives on Aggression Replacement Training* (pp. 153–170). Chichester, England: Wiley.

Goldstein, A. P. (2004b). Evaluations of effectiveness. In A. P. Goldstein, R. Nensen, B. Daleflod, & M. Kalt (Eds.), *New perspectives on Aggression Replacement Training* (pp. 231–244). Chichester, England: Wiley.

Goldstein, A. P., & Glick, B. (1987). *Aggression Replacement Training: A comprehensive intervention for adolescent youth.* Champaign, IL: Research Press.

Goldstein, A. P., Glick, B., & Gibbs, J. C. (1998). *Aggression Replacement Training: A comprehensive intervention for adolescent youth.* (Rev. ed.). Champaign, IL: Research Press.

Goldstein, A. P., & McGinnis, E. (1997). *Skillstreaming the elementary school child: New strategies and perspectives for teaching prosocial skills.* Champaign, IL: Research Press.

Goldstein, A. P., Nensen, R., Daleflod, B., & Kalt, M. (Eds.). (2004). *New perspectives on Aggression Replacement Training.* Chichester, England: Wiley.

Goleman, D. (2005). *Emotional intelligence: Why it can matter more than IQ.* New York: Random House.

Goodman, S. H., Gravitt, G. W., & Kaslow, N. J. (1995). Social problem solving: A moderator of the relationship between negative life stress and depression symptoms in children. *Journal of Abnormal Psychology, 23,* 473–485.

Gundersen, K., Strømgren, B., & moynahan, l. (2013). *Social Perception Training* (Prepare Curriculum Implementation Guide, M. Amendola & B. Oliver, Series Eds.). Champaign, IL: Research Press.

Hatcher, R. M., & Hollin, C. R. (2005). The identification and management of anti-social and offending behaviour. In J. Winstone & F. Pakes (Eds.), *Community justice: Issues for probation and community justice* (pp. 165–182). Cullompton, Devon: Willan Press.

Hollin, C. R. (1990). *Cognitive behavioral interventions with young offenders.* Elmsford, NY: Pergamon Press.

Hollin, C. R., & Bloxsom, C. A. J. (2007). Treatments for angry aggression. In T. A. Gannon, T. Ward, A. R. Beech, & D. Fisher (Eds.), *Aggressive offenders' cognition: Theory, research and practice* (pp. 215–229). Chichester, England: Wiley.

Hollin, C. R. & Palmer, E. J. (2001). Skills training. In C. R. Hollin (Ed.), *Handbook of offender assessment and treatment.* Chichester, England: John Wiley & Sons.

Hollin, C. R., & Palmer, E. J. (2006a). The Adolescent Problems Inventory: A profile of incarcerated English young male offenders. *Personality and Individual Differences, 40,* 1485–1495.

Hollin, C. R., & Palmer, E. J. (Eds). (2006b). *Offending behaviour programmes: Development, application, and controversies.* Chichester, England: Wiley.

Hollin, C. R., & Trower, P. (Eds.). (1986a). *Handbook of social skills training: Vol. 1. Applications across the life span.* Oxford, England: Pergamon Press.

Hollin, C. R., & Trower, P. (Eds.). (1986b). *Handbook of social skills training: Vol. 2. Clinical applications and new directions.* Oxford, England: Pergamon Press.

Horn, M., Shively, R., & Gibbs, J. C. (2007). *EQUIPPED for life game.* Westport, CT: Franklin Learning.

Johnson, D. W., Johnson, R. T., & Stanne, M. B. (2000). *Cooperative learning methods: A meta-analysis.* Cooperative Learning Center, University of Minnesota.

Jolliffe, D., & Farrington, D. P. (2007). Examining the relationship between low empathy and self-reported offending. *Legal and Criminological Psychology, 12,* 265–286.

Kohlberg, L. (1978). Revisions in the theory and practice of mental development. In W. Damon (Ed.), *New directions in child development: Moral development* (Vol. 2, pp. 83–88). San Francisco: Jossey-Bass.

Lipsey, M. W., & Wilson, D. B. (1998). Effective intervention for serious juvenile offenders. In R. Loeber & D. Farrington (Eds.), *Serious and violent juvenile offenders: Risk factors and successful interventions* (pp. 313–345). Thousand Oaks, CA: Sage.

Lipton, D. M., McDonel, E. C., & McFall, R. M. (1987). Heterosocial perception in rapists. *Journal of Consulting and Clinical Psychology, 55,* 17–21.

Lösel, F., & Beelmann, A. (2005). Social-problem-solving programs for preventing antisocial behavior in children and youth. In M. McMurran & J. McGuire (Eds.), *Social problem solving and offending: Evidence, evaluation, and evolution* (pp. 127–143). Chichester, England: Wiley.

Lösel, F., Bliesener, T., & Bender, D. (2007). Social information processing, experiences of aggression in social contexts, and aggressive behavior in adolescents. *Criminal Justice and Behavior, 34,* 330–347.

McCown, W., Johnson, J., & Austin, S. (1986). Inability of delinquents to recognize facial affects. *Journal of Social Behavior and Personality, 1,* 489–496.

McFall, R. (1982). A review and reformulation of the concept of social skills. *Behavioral Assessment, 4,* 1–33.

McGinnis, E., & Goldstein, A. P. (1997). *Skillstreaming the elementary school child: New strategies and perspectives for teaching prosocial skills* (Rev. ed.). Champaign, IL: Reseach Press.

McGuire, J. (2005). Social problem solving: Basic concepts, research, and applications. In M. McMurran (Ed.), *Social problem solving and offending: Evidence, evaluation, and evolution* (pp. 3–29). Chichester, England: Wiley.

McMurran, M. (2006). Drug and alcohol programmes: Concept, theory, and practice. In C. R. Hollin & E. J. Palmer (Eds.), *Offending behaviour programmes. Development, application, and controversies.* Chichester, England: Wiley.

Miller, P. A., & Eisenberg, N. (1988). The relation of empathy to aggressive and externalizing/antisocial behaviour. *Psychological Bulletin, 103,* 324–344.

moynahan, l. (2003). Enhanced Aggression Replacement Training with children and youth with autism spectrum disorder. *Reclaiming Children and Youth 12*(3), 174–180.

Muuss, R. E. (1960). The relationship between "causal" orientation, anxiety, and insecurity in elementary school children. *Journal of Educational Psychology, 51,* 122–129.

Nelson, J. R., Smith, D. J., & Dodd, J. (1990). The moral reasoning of juvenile delinquents: A meta-analysis. *Journal of Abnormal Child Psychology, 18,* 709–727.

Nezu, A. M., & Perri, M. (1989). Social problem therapy for unipolar depression: An initial dismantling investigation. *Journal of Consulting and Clinical Psychology, 57*(3), 408–413.

Nezu, A. M., & Ronan, G. F. (1987). Social problem solving and depression: Deficits in generating alternatives and decision making. *Southern Psychologist, 3,* 29–34.

Nezu, A. M., Wilkins, V. M., & Maguth-Nezu, C. (2004). Social problem solving stress and negative affect. In E. C. Chang, T. J. D'Zurilla, & L. J. Sanna (Eds.), *Social problem solving theory, research and training* (pp. 52–53). Washington, DC: American Psychological Association.

Nietzel, M. T., Hasemann, D. M., & Lynam, D. R. (1999). Behavioral perspective on violent behavior. In V. B. Van Hasselt & M. Hersen (Eds.), *Handbook of psychological approaches with violent offenders: Contemporary strategies and issues* (pp. 39-66). New York: Kluwer Academic/Plenum.

Novaco, R. W. (1975). *Anger control: The development and evaluation of an experimental treatment.* Lexington, MA: D. C. Heath.

Novaco, R. W. (2007). Anger dysregulation. In T. Cavell & K. Malcolm (Eds.), *Anger, aggression, and interventions for interpersonal violence* (pp. 3–54). Mahwah, NJ: Erlbaum.

Novaco, R. W., & Welsh, W. N. (1989). Anger disturbances: Cognitive mediation and clinical prescriptions. In K. Howells & C. R. Hollin (Eds.), *Clinical approaches to violence.* Chichester, England: Wiley.

Palmer, E. J. (2003). *Offending behaviour: Moral reasoning, criminal conduct and the rehabilitation of offenders.* Cullompton: Willan.

Palmer, E. J., & Hollin, C. R. (1999). Social competence and sociomoral reasoning in young offenders. *Applied Cognitive Psychology, 13,* 79–87.

Piaget, J. (1932). *The moral judgement of the child.* London: Routledge and Kegan Paul.

Potter, G. B., Gibbs, J., Goldstein, A. P. (2001). *The EQUIP implementation guide: Teaching youth to think and act responsibly through a peer-helping approach.* Champaign, IL: Research Press.

Ratey, J. (2008). *SPARK: The revolutionary new science of exercise and the brain.* New York: Little, Brown.

Schmitt, B. D. (1999). *Your child's health.* New York: Bantam.

Sellæg, N. J., Sætrang, G., & Wroldsen, P. (1993). *Speilbilder, om dagdrøm og livskunst* [Reflections, the reverie and art of living]. Oslo, Norway: Cappelen.

Shure, M. B. (2001). *I Can Problem Solve: An interpersonal cognitive problem-solving program* (Intermediate Elementary Grades). Champaign, IL: Research Press.

Spence, S. H. (1981a). Differences in social skills performance between institutionalized juvenile male offenders and a comparable group of boys without offence records. *British Journal of Clinical Psychology, 20,* 163–171.

Spence, S. H. (1981b). Validation of social skills of adolescent males in an interview conversation with a previously unknown adult. *Journal of Applied Behavior Analysis, 14,* 159–168.

Spivack, G., Platt, J. J., & Shure, M. B. (1976). *The problem-solving approach to adjustment.* San Francisco: Jossey-Bass.

Spivak, G., & Shure, M. B. (1974). *Social adjustment of young children.* San Francisco: Jossey-Bass.

Stams, G. J., Brugman, D., Dekovic, M., van Rosmale, L., van der Laan, P., & Gibbs, J. C. (2006). The moral judgment of juvenile delinquents: A meta-analysis. *Journal of Abnormal Child Psychology, 34,* 697–713.

Sukhodolsky, D. G., Golub, A., Stone, E. C., & Orban, L. (2005). Dismantling Anger Control Training for children: A randomizied pilot study of social problem-solving versus social skills training components. *Behavior Therapy, 36*(1), 15–23.

Swaffer, T., & Hollin, C. R. (2000). Anger and impulse control. In R. Newell & K. Gournay (Eds.), *Mental health nursing: An evidence-based approach* (pp. 265–289). Edinburgh: Churchill Livingstone.

Swaffer, T., & Hollin, C. R. (2001). Anger and general health in young offenders. *Journal of Forensic Psychiatry, 12,* 90–103.

Tate, D. C., Reppucci, N. D., & Mulvey, E. P. (1995). Violent juvenile delinquents: Treatment effectiveness and implications for future action. *American Psychologist, 50,* 777–781.

Thompson, P., & White, S. (2010). Play and positive group dynamics. *Reclaiming Children and Youth, 19*(3), 53–57.

Tsang, H. W. H., & Pearson, V. (2001). Work-related social skills training for people with schizophrenia in Hong Kong. *Schizophrenia Bulletin, 27*(1), 139–148.

Tuckman, B. W. (1965). Developmental sequences in small groups. *Psychological Bulletin, 63,* 384–399.

Tuckman, B. W., & Jensen, M. A. (1977). Stages of small group development revisited. *Group and Organization, 2,* 419–427.

Ucok, A., Cakir, S., Duman, Z. C., Discigil, A., Kandemir, P., & Atli, H. (2006). Cognitive predictors of skill acquisition on social problem solving in patients with schizophrenia. *European Archives of Psychiatry and Clinical Neuroscience, 256*(6), 388–394.

Ward, C. I., & McFall, R. M. (1986). Further validation of the Problem Inventory for Adolescent Girls: Comparing Caucasian and black delinquents and nondelinquents. *Journal of Consulting and Clinical Psychology, 54,* 732–733.

About the Editors

MARK AMENDOLA, LCW, started his career as a child care counselor at a residential treatment center in 1980 after earning a bachelor's degree from Gannon University in Erie, Pennsylvania. He served in a variety of roles, including counseling with delinquent youth in a day treatment program and as a mental health therapist and supervisor in a partial hospitalization program. He worked for Erie County, Pennsylvania, as a supervisor, authorizing treatment and providing quality management for residential and community-based programming. He has served as Executive Director of Perseus House, Inc., and Charter School of Excellence in Erie, Pennsylvania, since 1994 and 2002, respectively. He completed his graduate degree from Case Western University in 1990 and maintains a private practice that serves youth and adults.

ROBERT OLIVER, EdD, started his career as a child care counselor in an intensive treatment unit for delinquent youth. He spent multiple years as a mental health specialist and then worked in the capacity of supervisor of a partial hospitalization program. He began working in the school district of the City of Erie in 1989, serving as Principal of Alternative Education, Supervisor of Student Assistance Programs, Dean of Northwest Pennsylvania Collegiate Academy, Director of High Schools, and Assistant Superintendent. He is currently the Chief Educational Officer of the Perseus House Charter School of Excellence in Erie, Pennsylvania.

❧❧❧

Mark Amendola and Robert Oliver are partners in Education and Treatment Alternatives, an organization that provides national and international training in Aggression Replacement Training and Prepare Curriculum topics.

About the Authors

After graduating from Eastern Canada's Acadia University, KIM PARKER began a 30-year career working with youth in Montreal. When Aggression Replacement Training was first introduced at Batshaw Youth and Family Centres in Montreal, Kim became involved immediately. She began work with Family TIES groups at their inception and was instrumental in the creation of an agency-wide ART implementation plan. As a master trainer of the Prepare Curriculum elements and as the ART programming specialist at Batshaw, Kim provides support for ART through program development, animation, training, and coaching. In addition, she has been responsible for the collection of evaluation data. At the elementary school level, she has developed a conflict resolution program that incorporates Skillstreaming into other established programs. Kim acts frequently as a consultant and trainer on Problem-Solving Training and Prepare Curriculum components internationally. In partnership with Robert Calame, Kim has had a book and numerous articles published on Family TIES. In 2007, Kim was honored as Youth Care Worker of the Year by the Quebec Association of Educators. In 2008, Kim was recipient of the Ruth and Manny Batshaw Award of Excellence for her significant contributions in the field of child and youth care.

ROBERT CALAME is the former Coordinator of Aggression Replacement Training Programming at Batshaw Youth and Family Centres in Montreal, where he worked for over 30 years. The agency has had over 35 separate applications of ART in operation, as well as the adaptation for families referred to as Family TIES. Robert's social work background includes an undergraduate degree and graduate studies from the McGill University School of Social Work. His relevant interests are research geared toward improving generalization of competencies of the Prepare Curriculum and Aggression Replacement Training while working with families of youth in training. As a master trainer of the elements of the Prepare Curriculum, Robert offers training and consultation internationally in Dr. Goldstein's Prepare Curriculum topics in the form of workshops titled "Teaching Pro-social Behavior to Troubled Youth," acts as secretary of the advisory board for PREPSEC (PRepare for Evidence-based Practice in Social Emotional Competency) International, and is former secretary of the Quebec Association of Educators. With the help of coauthor Kim Parker, Robert has had a book, articles, and chapters published on the topic of Family TIES and Batshaw's work with ART and Prepare Curriculum components. In 2007, he was presented with a certificate of meritorious achievement for dedication and achievement in the field of child and youth care by the selection committee for the Ruth and Manny Batshaw Award of Excellence.

KNUT KORNELIUS GUNDERSEN is a professor at the Centre for Social Competence at Diakonhjemmet University College, Sandnes, Norway. He has written several books and scientific articles in the area of social competence, environmental therapy, and social networking. He has presented at national and international congresses in 14 different countries and is one of the key persons involved in the training and implementation of ART and Prepare Curriculum components in Norway, Iceland, Finland, Denmark, and Russia. President of the PRepare for Evidence-based Practice in Social Emotional Competency (PREPSEC) International board, he has also been an active member of the European Network for Social and Emotional Competence (ENSEC) organization, which targets the development of social and emotional competency via a European network of experts. He is first author of the *Social Perception Training* Prepare Curriculum Implementation Guide, forthcoming from Research Press.

ANDREW SIMON began his career as a stress management instructor in Montreal, which led him to working, for the past 26 years, for Batshaw Youth and Family Centres. In 2000, Andy became team leader of a residential treatment unit for adolescents, where he has been largely responsible for the development and implementation of a crisis intervention program for youth based largely on Problem-Solving Training. Since 2003, he has been a master trainer in Problem-Solving Training and other components of the Prepare Curriculum. Aside from training Batshaw staff in ART facilitation, Andy has been involved in teaching social competencies to Cree Social Services in Northern Quebec. He lives north of Montreal, where he has been involved in various community projects, including writing a column on parenting for the *Laurentian Sun*.

JOHN C. CHOI started his professional life working in community settings with children and families. Upon completion of his psychology degree at McGill University, he joined Batshaw Youth and Family Centres in Montreal, as well as established his own private practice, Mentoring Services. Using his passion to learn and teach, John contributed to the field of child and youth care and became a master trainer of the Prepare Curriculum elements, in particular, Problem-Solving Training. John also has developed expertise as a Peace Circle Keeper and a RAP/Circle of Courage Trainer. John was the 2011 recipient of the Lewis Peace Prize and since has become an onsite manager at Batshaw. He hopes to make further contributions to the field of child and youth care, health and social services, and, of course, to the youth and families he serves in his community in Quebec.

MARK AMENDOLA, LCW, started his career as a child care counselor at a residential treatment center in 1980 after earning a bachelor's degree from Gannon University in Erie, Pennsylvania. He served in a variety of roles, including counseling with delinquent youth in a day treatment program and as a mental health therapist and supervisor in a partial hospitalization program. He worked for Erie County, Pennsylvania, as a supervisor, authorizing treatment and providing quality management for residential and community-based programming. He has served as Executive Director of Perseus House, Inc., and Charter School of Excellence in Erie, Pennsylvania, since 1994 and 2002, respectively. He completed his graduate degree from Case Western University in 1990 and maintains a private practice that serves youth and adults.